Intelligent Computing for Big Data

Intelligent Computing for Big Data

Editors
Wei Wang
Ka Lok Man

MDPI • Basel • Beijing • Wuhan • Barcelona • Belgrade • Manchester • Tokyo • Cluj • Tianjin

Editors
Wei Wang
Xi'an Jiaotong-Liverpool
University
China

Ka Lok Man
Xi'an Jiaotong-Liverpool
University
China

Editorial Office
MDPI
St. Alban-Anlage 66
4052 Basel, Switzerland

This is a reprint of articles from the Special Issue published online in the open access journal *Applied Sciences* (ISSN 2076-3417) (available at: https://www.mdpi.com/journal/applsci/special_issues/Intelligent_Computing_Big_Data).

For citation purposes, cite each article independently as indicated on the article page online and as indicated below:

LastName, A.A.; LastName, B.B.; LastName, C.C. Article Title. *Journal Name* **Year**, *Volume Number*, Page Range.

ISBN 978-3-0365-5877-6 (Hbk)
ISBN 978-3-0365-5878-3 (PDF)

© 2022 by the authors. Articles in this book are Open Access and distributed under the Creative Commons Attribution (CC BY) license, which allows users to download, copy and build upon published articles, as long as the author and publisher are properly credited, which ensures maximum dissemination and a wider impact of our publications.

The book as a whole is distributed by MDPI under the terms and conditions of the Creative Commons license CC BY-NC-ND.

Contents

About the Editors . . . . **vii**

Wei Wang and Ka Lok Man
Special Issue on Intelligent Computing for Big Data
Reprinted from: *Appl. Sci.* **2022**, *12*, 11106, doi:10.3390/app122111106 . . . . **1**

Maraheb Alsuliman and Heyam H. Al-Baity
Efficient Diagnosis of Autism with Optimized Machine Learning Models: An Experimental
Analysis on Genetic and Personal Characteristic Datasets
Reprinted from: *Appl. Sci.* **2022**, *12*, 3812, doi:10.3390/app12083812 . . . . **3**

Jinah Kim and Nammee Moon
Dog Behavior Recognition Based on Multimodal Data from a Camera and Wearable Device
Reprinted from: *Appl. Sci.* **2022**, *12*, 3199, doi:10.3390/app12063199 . . . . **25**

Byoungwook Kim, Yeongwook Yang, Ji Su Park and Hong-Jun Jang
A Convolution Neural Network-Based Representative Spatio-Temporal Documents
Classification for Big Text Data
Reprinted from: *Appl. Sci.* **2022**, *12*, 3843, doi:10.3390/app12083843 . . . . **43**

Hsien-Ming Chou
A Smart-Mutual Decentralized System for Long-Term Care
Reprinted from: *Appl. Sci.* **2022**, *12*, 3664, doi:10.3390/app12073664 . . . . **57**

Jia Kan, Jie Zhang, Dawei Liu and Xin Huang
Proxy Re-Encryption Scheme for Decentralized Storage Networks
Reprinted from: *Appl. Sci.* **2022**, *12*, 4260, doi:10.3390/app12094260 . . . . **71**

About the Editors

Wei Wang

Dr. Wei Wang is a Senior Associate Professor at the Department of Computing, School of Advanced Technology, Xi'an Jiaotong-Liverpool University, China. After receiving his PhD in Computer Science from the University of Nottingham in 2009, he worked as a Lecturer at the University of Nottingham (Malaysia Campus), and later, as a Post-Doctoral Research Fellow at the Centre for Communication Systems Research (now known as the Institute for Communication Systems) at the University of Surrey, UK. His research interests lie in the broad area of data and knowledge engineering; in particular, he is interested in knowledge discovery, intelligent computing, and deep learning for data processing. He has published more than 60 papers in reputed journals and conferences in the areas of knowledge discovery, machine learning, data mining and the Internet of Things.

Ka Lok Man

Ka Lok Man is currently a Professor at the School of Advanced Technology, Xi'an Jiaotong-Liverpool University (XJTLU), Suzhou, China, and an Honorary Recognised Professor at the Department of Computer Science, the University of Liverpool, UK. He is an External PhD supervisor at the Department of Computer Science, KU, Leuven, Belgium. He is also an Honorary Recognised Professor at the Big Data Excellence Centre, Kazimieras Simonavičius University, Lithuania and a Visiting Professor at the Faculty of Informatics, Vytautas Magnus University, Lithuania. He has approximately 20 years of international teaching experience and several years of industrial experience in integrated circuit design, and has been engaged in many industry-oriented research projects in Microelectronics and Computer Science, many of them in cooperation with STMicroelectronics, Synopsys, and LG. He has a good publication record, having published more than 500 academic articles to date. Additionally, he has received more than 50 international research awards and fellowships.

Editorial

Special Issue on Intelligent Computing for Big Data

Wei Wang * and Ka Lok Man

Department of Computing, School of Advanced Technology, Xi'an Jiaotong-Liverpool University, Suzhou 215123, China
* Correspondence: wei.wang03@xjtlu.edu.cn; Tel.: +86-512-88167736

1. Introduction

Passion for a classic research area of computer science, artificial intelligence (AI), has experienced new momentum in recent years. This is largely inspired by the astonishing developments of deep learning research, whose success has been shown in computer vision [1] and natural language processing [2]. Developed models and techniques for intelligent computing have also been adopted in numerous real-world applications for data processing, for example, social media [3], natural language texts [4] and Internet of Things [5], to name just a few. Research on big data processing and analytics has achieved considerable success in recent decades. Nevertheless, the promise of allowing the extraction of valuable information and trustworthy knowledge from a tremendous amount of data of various forms and modalities has yet to come true.

2. Applications for Intelligent Computing for Big Data

Recent advances in AI research have the potential to move current big data research one step further. In light of this, this Special Issue, 'Intelligent Computing for Big Data', was proposed to collect the latest research and applications related to the use of relevant intelligent computing techniques to process big data. The Special Issue has accepted five papers for publication.

The paper by Jinah Kim and Nammee Moon [6] proposes a deep neural network for fusing multimodal data, e.g., video and sensor data, for dog behaviour recognition. The objective of the work is to minimise and compensate for noise presented in collected real-time data. Evaluation studies show that the best performance of the model was achieved when multimodal data were used. The paper by Hsien-Ming Chou [7] aims to address the important and timely problem of long-term elderly care using a decentralised architecture with blockchain technologies. Based on the identified challenges of the current systems, the author proposes the mapping mutual clustering algorithm, which has the potential to alleviate the issues of mental alienation, insufficient manpower, and privacy. A post-study questionnaire shows that a high level of forecasting accuracy and positive user perception can be achieved. The paper by Maraheb Alsuliman and Heyam H. Al-Baity [8] presents a comprehensive experimental study on use of traditional supervised learning and feature selection algorithms in the early diagnosis of autism. With bio-inspired feature selection algorithms, impressive classification accuracy can be obtained on gene expression as well as personal and behavioural data. The study has valuable practical implications for researchers and practitioners working on early the detection of autism disorder. The work presented by Byoungwook Kim et al. [9] attempts to extract spatiotemporal information from online big text data for event analysis. A new character-level convolutional neural network-based model that is specifically designed to extract spatio-temporal information describing the core subjects of documents is proposed to classify representative spatio-temporal documents. The work by Jia Kan et al. [10] addresses an important problem of big data storage and cryptographic access control in decentralised storage networks, i.e., permission-less blockchains. They propose a new and efficient chosen ciphertext attack-secure and collusion-resilient proxy re-encryption scheme for decentralised storage. The scheme has the potential to be used in many blockchain applications, e.g., online stores for digital products.

3. Future Research

The papers in this Special Issue only cover a very limited number of topics and applications of intelligent computing for big data. More in-depth theoretical and practical research in this converged area of artificial intelligence and big data is anticipated. It is expected that more techniques and algorithms will be designed along with some interesting and exciting future directions such as zero short learning, neurosymbolic learning, the fusion of large-scale knowledge graphs, and knowledge reusability and transferability.

Acknowledgments: This Special Issue would have not been possible without the great contributions from the authors, reviewers, and professional editorial team at *Applied Sciences*, MDPI. First, we would like to say congratulations to all authors whose manuscripts have been accepted by this Special Issue for publication. We would like to take this opportunity to express our sincere gratefulness to all reviewers for their valuable feedback, comments, and suggestions, which have helped the authors further improve the quality of the submissions. Last but not least, we would like to express our gratitude to the editorial team of *Applied Sciences* for the timely help, efficient work, and professionalism. The work is partially supported by 2022 Jiangsu Science and Technology Programme (General Programme), contract number BK20221260.

Conflicts of Interest: The authors declare no conflict of interest.

References

1. LeCun, Y.; Bengio, Y.; Hinton, G. Deep learning. *Nature* **2015**, *521*, 436–444. [CrossRef] [PubMed]
2. Brown, T.B.; Mann, B.; Ryder, N.; Subbiah, M.; Kaplan, J.D.; Dhariwal, P.; Neelakantan, A.; Shyam, P.; Sastry, G.; Askell, A.; et al. Language models are few-shot learners. In Proceedings of the 34th International Conference on Neural Information Processing Systems (NIPS'20), Vancouver, BC, Canada, 6–12 December 2020; Curran Associates Inc.: Red Hook, NY, USA, 2020; Article 159, pp. 1877–1901.
3. Chen, Q.; Wang, W.; Huang, K.; Coenen, F. Zero-shot Text Classifi- cation via Knowledge Graph Embedding for Social Media Data. *IEEE Internet Things J.* **2021**, *9*, 9205–9213. [CrossRef]
4. Dong, H.; Wang, W.; Huang, K.; Coenen, F. Automated Social Text Annotation with Joint Multi-Label Attention Networks. *IEEE Trans. Neural Netw. Learn. Syst.* **2020**, *32*, 2224–2238. [CrossRef] [PubMed]
5. Chen, Q.; Wang, W.; Wu, F.; De, S.; Wang, R.; Zhang, B.; Huang, X. A Survey on an Emerging Area: Deep Learning for Smart City Data. *IEEE Trans. Emerg. Top. Comput. Intell.* **2019**, *3*, 392–410. [CrossRef]
6. Kim, J.; Moon, N. Dog Behavior Recognition Based on Multimodal Data from a Camera and Wearable Device. *Appl. Sci.* **2022**, *12*, 3199. [CrossRef]
7. Chou, H. A Smart-Mutual Decentralized System for Long-Term Care. *Appl. Sci.* **2022**, *12*, 3664. [CrossRef]
8. Alsuliman, M.; Al-Baity, H. Efficient Diagnosis of Autism with Optimized Machine Learning Models: An Experimental Analysis on Genetic and Personal Characteristic Datasets. *Appl. Sci.* **2022**, *12*, 3812. [CrossRef]
9. Kim, B.; Yang, Y.; Park, J.; Jang, H. A Convolution Neural Network-Based Representative Spatio-Temporal Documents Classification for Big Text Data. *Appl. Sci.* **2022**, *12*, 3843. [CrossRef]
10. Kan, J.; Zhang, J.; Liu, D.; Huang, X. Proxy Re-Encryption Scheme for Decentralized Storage Networks. *Appl. Sci.* **2022**, *12*, 4260. [CrossRef]

Article

Efficient Diagnosis of Autism with Optimized Machine Learning Models: An Experimental Analysis on Genetic and Personal Characteristic Datasets

Maraheb Alsuliman [1,*] and Heyam H. Al-Baity [2]

1. IT Department, College of Computing and Informatics, Saudi Electronic University, Riyadh 11673, Saudi Arabia
2. IT Department, College of Computer and Information Sciences, King Saud University, Riyadh 11543, Saudi Arabia; halbaity@ksu.edu.sa
* Correspondence: ma.alsuliman@seu.edu.sa

Abstract: Early diagnosis of autism is extremely beneficial for patients. Traditional diagnosis approaches have been unable to diagnose autism in a fast and accurate way; rather, there are multiple factors that can be related to identifying the autism disorder. The gene expression (GE) of individuals may be one of these factors, in addition to personal and behavioral characteristics (PBC). Machine learning (ML) based on PBC and GE data analytics emphasizes the need to develop accurate prediction models. The quality of prediction relies on the accuracy of the ML model. To improve the accuracy of prediction, optimized feature selection algorithms are applied to solve the high dimensionality problem of the datasets used. Comparing different optimized feature selection methods using bio-inspired algorithms over different types of data can allow for the most accurate model to be identified. Therefore, in this paper, we investigated enhancing the classification process of autism spectrum disorder using 16 proposed optimized ML models (GWO-NB, GWO-SVM, GWO-KNN, GWO-DT, FPA-NB, FPA-KNN, FPA-SVM, FPA-DT, BA-NB, BA-SVM, BA-KNN, BA-DT, ABC-NB, ABC-SVM, ABV-KNN, and ABC-DT). Four bio-inspired algorithms namely, Gray Wolf Optimization (GWO), Flower Pollination Algorithm (FPA), Bat Algorithms (BA), and Artificial Bee Colony (ABC), were employed for optimizing the wrapper feature selection method in order to select the most informative features and to increase the accuracy of the classification models. Five evaluation metrics were used to evaluate the performance of the proposed models: accuracy, F1 score, precision, recall, and area under the curve (AUC). The obtained results demonstrated that the proposed models achieved a good performance as expected, with accuracies of 99.66% and 99.34% obtained by the GWO-SVM model on the PBC and GE datasets, respectively.

Keywords: autism spectrum disorder (ASD); big data; bioinformatics; machine learning; classification; bio-inspired algorithms; Grey Wolf Optimization (GWO); Support Vector Machine (SVM)

Citation: Alsuliman, M.; Al-Baity, H.H. Efficient Diagnosis of Autism with Optimized Machine Learning Models: An Experimental Analysis on Genetic and Personal Characteristic Datasets. *Appl. Sci.* 2022, 12, 3812. https://doi.org/10.3390/app12083812

Academic Editor: Wei Wang

Received: 8 March 2022
Accepted: 5 April 2022
Published: 10 April 2022

Publisher's Note: MDPI stays neutral with regard to jurisdictional claims in published maps and institutional affiliations.

Copyright: © 2022 by the authors. Licensee MDPI, Basel, Switzerland. This article is an open access article distributed under the terms and conditions of the Creative Commons Attribution (CC BY) license (https://creativecommons.org/licenses/by/4.0/).

1. Introduction

Autism spectrum disorder (ASD) is a neurological developmental disorder. It affects how people connect and interact with others and how they behave and learn [1]. The symptoms and signs appear when a child is very young. It is a lifelong condition and cannot be cured. Today, ASD is one of the fastest-growing developmental disorders, resulting in many problems, such as school problems related to successful learning, psychological stress within the family, and social isolation. However, early diagnosis can help the family take preliminary and effective steps to ensure the normal life of the patient. It can help providers of healthcare and families of patients by affording the effective therapy and treatment required, thereby reducing the costs associated with delayed diagnosis. On the other hand, many factors can be used to detect ASD cases, including personal and behavioral characteristics, genetic, brain images, and family history. Notwithstanding its genetic causes, ASD is mainly diagnosed utilizing personal and behavioral indicators that are tested in traditional clinical examinations by different specialists during regular visits. However, these traditional clinical methods, which primarily depend on the clinician, are time consuming and cumbersome. Currently, with computer power and big data generated by hospitals such as clinical data, gene expression profiles, and medical imaging, ASD can be automatically predicted and diagnosed in its early stages by using predictive models that use big data sets with ML algorithms, which can improve the life quality of patients and families as well as reduce the financial costs.

The personal and behavioral characteristics (PBC) and the gene expression (GE) data are the most available and valuable resources for machine learning (ML) algorithms seeking to discover new and hidden patterns of data to help in ASD prediction, thus helping families to take early steps for treatment. Nevertheless, the high dimensionality of these data makes the prediction process challenging. The feature selection (FS) mechanism can help in reducing the high dimensionality of such datasets, increasing the speed of the classification process, decreasing the cost, and improving the accuracy of the prediction models by selecting the most effective features.

Feature selection algorithms [2] aim to choose the most significant features to solve the prediction problems. In general, there are three common types of FS algorithm: filter, wrapper, and hybrid. Due to the potential benefits that can be achieved from automatic ASD classification, research in this field has recently gained much attention. Several methods have been proposed to solve the problem of predicting ASD. However, it is still an open problem and further improvement can be achieved.

Bio-inspired algorithms are one of the techniques that can be integrated into the wrapper feature selection method to search globally for the optimal feature subset and improve prediction accuracy [3]. They can be classified as a type of Nature-inspired Computation algorithms that rely on the inspiration of the biological evolution of nature to provide new optimization techniques. A number of researchers have adopted bio-inspired techniques for dealing with the high dimensionality of features, and they have shown high results in improving the diagnosis process of many diseases such as cancer [4]. However, there are few studies in research on ASD prediction using optimized FS algorithms and further investigation in this field is needed. To the best of our knowledge, this is the first study to deal with this problem using four bio-inspired algorithms (GWO, FPA, BA, and ABC). In addition, this is the first study that employed the CNN deep learning approach for ASD GE and PBC datasets.

This work aims to enhance the accuracy of early prediction of ASD and the classification performance when dealing with high-dimensional datasets by developing a ML predictive model that is based on an optimized feature selection method using bio-inspired algorithms. This can be accomplished by conducting a comparative empirical study using four bio-inspired algorithms incorporated in four ML algorithms on two ASD datatypes, PBC and GE. Thus, this work proposes 16 optimized ML models named GWO-NB, GWO-SVM, GWO-KNN, GWO-DT, FPA-NB, FPA-KNN, FPA-SVM, FPA-DT, BA-NB, BA-SVM, BA-KNN, BA-DT, ABC-NB, ABC-SVM, ABV-KNN, and ABC-DT. This work is going to answer the following research questions:

1. Is the proposed bio-inspired-based wrapper feature selection method able to enhance the accuracy results of ML classifiers in ASD prediction?
2. Which one of the proposed 16 optimized models will give the best performance in ASD prediction in terms of accuracy and on which dataset?
3. What is the type of dataset (PBC and GE) that will give the best accuracy result for predicting ASD?
4. Will the deep learning approach give better results in the ASD prediction problem on PBC and GE datasets compared to the proposed bio-inspired-based wrapper feature selection method?

The rest of this paper is organized as follows: Section II describes the background; Section III is about related work; Section IV presents the materials and methodology of our work; Section V discusses the experimental results; and, finally, Section VI concludes the paper and shows some of our future work.

2. Background

2.1. Personal and Behavioral Characteristics (PBC)

At clinical diagnosis, clinicians use questionnaires and behavioral observation to collect personal and behavioral information based on the Manual of Mental Disorders (DSM-5) criteria, which include two main symptoms. The first symptom is a chronic deficiency in social communication and social engagement through various contexts. The second symptom is minimal and repeated behavior patterns, desires, and behaviors. Personal and behavioral data generally include tens of attributes (high dimensionality) that can be classified into personal information (such as age, ethnicity, and born with jaundice) and behavioral screening questions (such as "Do ASD patients often hear small sounds when others do not?" or "Is it difficult to hold the attention of ASD patients?") [5].

2.2. Gene Expression Profile (GE)

Gene expression is the mechanism by which the information stored in the gene is used to guide the assembly of the protein molecules. DNA microarray technology has become an effective way of tracking gene expression levels within the organism for biologists [6]. This technique helps researchers to assess the expression levels of a set of genes. Gene expression data usually comprise a wide range of genes and a small number of samples (high dimensionality). In medical fields, microarray technology is most widely used to find out what reasons and how to cure illnesses. Researchers have found that often the cause of some diseases, such as ASD, may be DNA mutations. It is well known that certain disorders are caused by the mutation of certain known genes. There is however, no particular form of mutation that causes all disorders. Therefore, the microarray gene expression analysis is used to identify and diagnose common genes mutations. Analysis of GE data is the method of identifying the helpful genes in the diagnosis.

2.3. Classification Algorithms

In our work, we used four different classification algorithms to analyze the datasets: support vector machine (SVM), decision tree (DT), Naïve Bayes (NB), and k-nearest neighbor (KNN) algorithms.

SVM [7] is one of the classification algorithms, and classifies two data types: linear and nonlinear.

First, the training dataset is converted into a higher dimension using nonlinear mapping. Next, it looks for linear separating hyperplanes (which are decision boundaries that help classify the data points) in the new dimension and splits the data based on the class. The optimal hyperplane [7] separates data points into classes that can be specified based on margin and support vectors. Support vectors are identified as the closest points of each class to the margin line. The NB classifier is based on Bayes' theorem and is a probabilistic classifier. The presumption of conditional independence underpins this classifier. This implies that the values of the attributes for each class mark are effectively conditionally independent of one another. Despite this basic assumption, Naïve Bayes has been successfully applied to a variety of real-world data circumstances [8]. KNN is a simple, easy-to-implement supervised machine learning algorithm that can be used to solve both classification and regression problems. It is based on the similarity measure to classify the new cases by calculating the distance measured from the trained available cases. In DT, the data are visualized using a tree structure, which is represented as sequences and consequences using the decision tree. The root node is at the top of the tree, while the internal nodes are where the attributes are tested. The result of the test is represented by the "branch". Finally, leaf nodes are nodes that have no further branching and indicate the class label of all previous decisions.

2.4. Feature Selection (FS)

Feature selection, as a data preprocessing technique, has been shown to be effective and efficient in preparing high-dimensional data for ML problems. The objectives of the selection of features include the development of simpler and more comprehensible models, the improvement of ML efficiency, and the preparation of clean and understandable data. The recent proliferation of large data has posed some major challenges and opportunities for feature selection algorithms [9]. The most common feature selection techniques are as follows: The filter approach, where the typical features are ranked via specific criteria. Features are then identified with the highest ratings then used as inputs for the wrapping or classification process [8,10]. On the other hand, the definition of the wrapper method requires the use of learning strategies to choose the optimum function subset to be used in the classification process. Usually, the wrapper method uses nature-inspired computational algorithms (NICs) to direct the search process by choosing the optimum feature subsets. The third approach is hybrid, which uses both filter and wrapper approaches. Based on [11], feature selection is a difficult task due to the need for searching over a large space, which is impossible in some applications that have large features and small samples. This problem can be solved using NIC algorithms that are able to search globally and can be utilized to solve the feature selection problem.

2.5. Nature-Inspired Computation (NIC)

NIC [12] refers to algorithms that imitate or optimize the behavior of natural and biological systems to solve problems in order to overcome or optimize the limitations of certain algorithms. All these algorithms share two characteristics: natural phenomena are replicated and modelled. NIC algorithms can be categorized into four types: swarm intelligence, bio-inspired, physics and chemistry, and other algorithms [13].

2.6. Bio-Inspired Algorithms

This is an emerging approach, focused on the inspiration of the biological evolution of nature, to develop new competing techniques. Bio-inspired optimization algorithms have demonstrated greater performance in a variety of disciplines, including disease diagnosis, by using the wrapper technique to high-dimensional datasets for feature selection. Algorithms for bio-inspired optimization are usually classified into three categories. Some of the well-known bio-inspired algorithms are described in the following section and are shown in Figure 1.

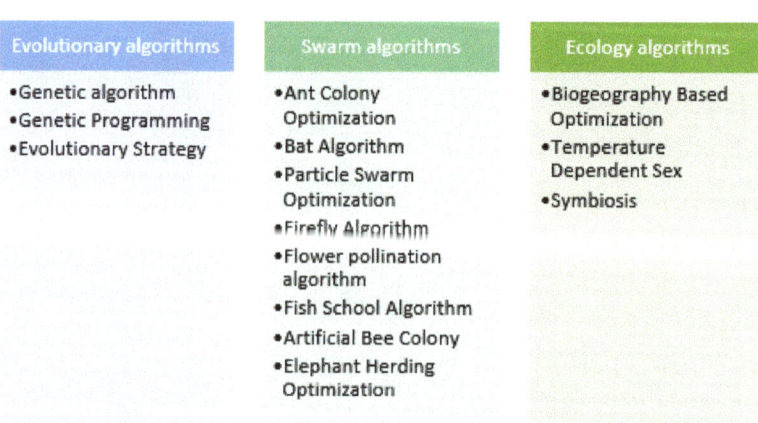

Figure 1. Bio-inspired algorithms.

2.7. Grey Wolf Optimization (GWO)

GWO algorithm is a recent algorithm proposed in 2014 [14]. This algorithm mimics the social behavior of grey wolves while searching and hunting for the prey. Normally, the wolves live in a pack with a group size of 5 to 12. The wolves are guided by three leaders, namely, alpha, beta, and delta wolves. The alpha wolf is responsible for making the decision, the beta wolf helps the alpha wolf in decision-making or pack activity, while the delta wolf submits to the alpha and beta, and dominates the omega wolves.

2.8. Bat Algorithms (BA)

This is one of the newest micro-bat algorithms, naturally inspired, utilizing echolocation behavior to locate their prey. To measure size, echolocation is used by bats. Therefore, in order to pick the booty (solution), they randomly migrate to particular locations at a given velocity and at a set frequency. Among the best solutions, the solution is selected and created through the use of random walking [15].

2.9. Flower Pollination Algorithms (FPA)

The flower pollination algorithm, one of the newest optimization algorithms, is inspired by the action of flower pollination. Crop pollination strategies in nature include two primary types: cross-pollination and self-pollination [16]. Some birds act as global pollinators in cross-pollination, passing pollen to the flowers of more distant plants. On the other hand, pollen is spread by the wind and only among adjacent flowers in the same plant during self-pollination. The FPA is therefore established by mapping the two types of cross-pollination and self-pollination into global pollination operators and local pollination operators. Due to the merits of fundamental principles, few parameters, and ease of operation, the FPA has attracted considerable interest.

2.10. Artificial Bee Colony (ABC)

This is an organic algorithm inspired essentially by the behavior of bees in the search for good sources of food. The ABC algorithm consists of three classes of bees: employed bees, onlooker bees, and scout bees. The employed bees find a source of food as well as exchange information of the source of food with the employed bees in the hive who are waiting for dancing. The onlooker bees choose a good source of food from the discovered food. The bees that choose the food sources at random are known as scout bees. Any bees that do not change their food source become scout bees [17].

3. Related Work

There are many well-known ASD datasets that have been widely used in the relevant literature. These datasets can be classified into three types: personal and behavioral characteristics datasets (PBC), gene expression datasets (GE), and MRI mages datasets. It has been noticed that most previous works that handled ASD prediction either used ML or DL methods. There are some studies that used ML to perform classification without incorporating any of the feature selection algorithms presented in Table 1, and others that used simple feature selection algorithms before classification presented in Table 2. Nevertheless, there are very limited studies that used optimization algorithms in order to enhance the selection process of optimal features before the classification step, which are presented in Table 3. On the other hand, there are a few studies that employed the DL approach to predict ASD using GE and MRI images, and we reviewed few of them in Table 4.

Accordingly, the proposed taxonomy of our review of literature is divided into two main subsections. First, ASD prediction using the ML approach, which includes studies without FS methods, studies with FS methods, and studies with optimized FS methods using bio-inspired algorithms, using three dataset types (PBC, GE, and MRI images). Second, ASD prediction using the DL approach.

Table 1. ASD prediction using ML without FS.

Data Type	Ref	ML Classifier	Classification Accuracy
PBC	[18]	KNN	67.5%
		LR	72%
		SVM	70.5%
		LDA	72.2%
		NB	70.7%
	[5]	K-NN	86.8%
		SVM	90.9%
		RF	99.5%
	[19]	K-NN	69.2%
		LR	68.60%
		RF	67.78%
	[20]	RF	55%
		SVC	62%
GE	[21]	SVM	93.7%
		K-NN	93.8%
		LDA	68.8%
	[22]	DT	98%
		SVM	96%
	[23]	RF	80%
MRI Images	[24]	RF	59%

Table 2. ASD prediction using ML with simple FS.

Data Type	Ref	FS	ML Classifier	Classification Accuracy
PBC	[25]	Chi Square	RT	94.9%
		RFE		95.2%
		CFS		93.5%
		IG		95.1%
		BT		95.7%
	[26]	Relief Attribute	SMO	100%
GE	[27]	IG	DT	53.3%
			K-NN	83.3%
			NB	86.67%
MRI Images	[28]	t-test filter LASSO logistic regression	SVM	76%
	[29]	RFE	RF	60%

Table 3. ASD prediction using ML with optimized FS.

Data Type	Ref	FS	ML Classifier	Classification Accuracy
PBC	[3]	Binary Firefly	NB	95.55%
			SVM	97.95%
			K-NN	93.84%

Table 3. *Cont.*

Data Type	Ref	FS	ML Classifier	Classification Accuracy
GE	[30]	(TT)+ (COR)+ (WRS)+ GBPSO	SVM	92.1%
	[31]	GA	RF	87%
MRI Images	[32]	PSO	SVM RF	81% 91%

Table 4. ASD prediction using DL.

Data Type	Ref	ML Classifier	Classification Accuracy
GE	[27]	DBN	98.64%
MRI Images	[33]	CNN	63%
	[34]	RNN	70.1%

3.1. ASD Prediction Using ML Approach

3.1.1. ASD Prediction Using ML without FS Methods

Bhawana et al. [18] tried to diagnose ASD by applying ML techniques on the personal and behavioral dataset. The k nearest neighbor (KNN), support vector machine (SVM), linear regression (LR), Naïve Bayes (NB), and linear discriminant analysis (LDA) algorithms have used in the classification. The result of the implementation shows that the LDA algorithm had the best result of 72.2% and was the most accurate compared with the other algorithms.

Likewise, Erkan et al. [5] developed an autism prediction model to classify ASD data. They used the KNN, SVM, and random forest (RF) ML classifiers. They performed their models for the clinical diagnosis of ASD of all ages on the basis of personal and behavioral characteristics. The results obtained indicate that the RF and SVM methods provided a high classification performance.

Furthermore, Devika et al. [19] focused on the development of some classification models using ML algorithms such as RF and LR algorithms, and the KNN algorithm with two datasets—adults and toddler. KNN has a higher accuracy score of 69.2% compared to the other two algorithms that are calculated in the experimental results which were 68% for LR and 67% for RF.

Hana et al. [20] used an existing dataset to implement a variety of ML methods. The aim was to test the accuracy of various approaches for abetter evaluation, and then to develop a model that would be used to predict children's autism. This was achieved by applying a standard autism test for infants, based on personal and behavioral assessments and widely used by psychologists and pediatricians to diagnose autism. The dataset contains 292 instances of children with 21 attributes. The RF and Support Vector Classifier (SVC) ML classifiers were applied, and the result was not satisfying—the highest accuracy was about 62%.

This study by Dong Hoon Oh et al. [21] used a gene expression profile to predict ASD. In this study, they used the published microarray data (GSE26415) from the Gene Expression Omnibus database, which included 21 young adults with ASD and 21 unaffected controls. SVM, K-NN, and LDA classifiers were used to assess the predictive model. The highest performance was for SVM and KNN.

In addition, supervised ML techniques were used by V. Pream et al. [22] to construct a model to diagnose ASD by classifying the genes that underlie this disease. To explore the results, they used SVM and DT. To validate the predictive results, a 10-fold cross-validation method was used. They found that, compared to SVM, the DT classifier performed better, with an accuracy of 94%.

Similarly, Muhammad Asif et al. in [23] developed a machine learning-based methodology for the identification of some disease genes, including ASD. They applied different ML classifiers such as NB, SVM, and RF. The results show RF had the highest accuracy with 80%.

The study by Gajendra et al. [24] shows that brain markers can be used for identifying ASD. The research focused on MRIs of children's (3–4 years) brains and achieved a high-grade success of 95% with an RF classifier. In addition, they showed that the growth of the autistic brain significantly decreases after the age of 3 years.

3.1.2. ASD Prediction Using ML with FS Methods

Shanthi et al. [25] compared several FS algorithms to classify ASD. They performed two experiments. First, with all features, they calculated the accuracy of the random tree (RT) classification algorithm and the result was 95.1%. Second, to improve the efficacy of the RT classifier, they used chi-square, correlation feature selection (CFS), bagged tree feature selector (BT), recursive feature elimination (RFE), subset evaluation, and information gain (IG). The optimal selection of each feature selection algorithm was assisted by a 10-fold cross-validation RT classification algorithm. The results show that the BT model with the RT classifier had a high accuracy of 95.7% compared with 95.2% for REF.

Muhammad et al. [26] analyzed four ASD datasets for toddler, child, adolescent, and adult. They applied different feature selection algorithms on ASD datasets such as relief feature, IG, and CS, and relief feature outperformed the others. They also used some classification techniques and the sequential minimal optimization (SMO) algorithm worked best for the detection of ASD cases for all of the ASD datasets. A 10-fold cross-validation method also was used to assess the datasets.

This study by Noura Samy et al. [27] used IG filter with three ML classifiers. They used gene expressing profiles to compere the performance of ML classifiers such as decision tree (DT), KNN, and NB after applied IG filter. The results showed that the Naïve Bayes had an accuracy of 86.67%, while the accuracy was 83% for KNN and 53% for DT.

Yan Jin et al. [28] proposed an SVM-based classification system that used brain images to classify 6-month-old infants at high risk for ASD. Two feature selection algorithms were performed. First, a t-test and followed by the LASSO logistic regression. LASSO logistic regression is a widely used feature selection algorithm that can pick a parsimonious collection of features from a wide range of potential candidates to improve the classification accuracy. It only maintains the most discriminatory features, thus discarding the obsolete ones. The outcome achieved an accuracy of 76%.

The purpose of a study by Gajendra et al. [29] was to solve high-dimensional and heterogeneous dataset problems like the Autism Brain Imaging Data Exchange (ABIDE) dataset. Previous works on the ABIDE dataset have reported accuracies less than 60%. In their study, they investigated the predictive power of MRI in ASD utilizing three classifiers: RF, SVM, and gradient boosting machine (GBM). They used RFE for the feature selection technique and the results showed that the classification accuracy could reach 60%.

3.1.3. ASD Prediction Using ML with Optimized FS Methods

There was only one study that used bio inspired algorithms on this data type. Vaishali et al. [3] tried to use the Firefly feature selection algorithm to improve ASD classification by providing a minimum set of features. The dataset contains 21 features, which makes it a high dimensional dataset. They used firefly feature selection algorithm with these classifiers (NB, SVM, and KNN) with 10-fold cross-validation, and they compared the accuracy before and after applying feature selection. The results show that the firefly feature selection algorithm selected 10 feature subsets among the 21 features in the dataset as optimum and the SVM classifier provided the highest score with 97.5%.

Hameed et al. [30] tried to improve the accuracy of the gene classification for ASD by using ML with geometric binary particle swarm optimization (GBPSO), which is one type of bio-inspired algorithm. They used different filters to reduce features to be 9454 features (genes). Then, they used statistical filters, which were as follows: the two-sample t-test (TT), the group correlation of features (COR) and the Wilcoxon rank sum test (WRS). The last step was choosing genes by using a GBPSO-SVM wrapper-based algorithm along with the used filters. The advantage of using this algorithm is because GBPSO starts with a random number of selected genes and searches in each iteration for the appropriate subset of genes. Then, 10-fold cross-validation with the SVM classifier was used to test the output of each candidate subset. The GBPSO algorithm contributed to the choice of an optimal subset of genes, offering the highest accuracy of classification. The combined gene subset selected by the GBPSO-SVM algorithm has been able to increase the accuracy of the classification to reach 92.1%.

Similarly, Tomasz et al. [31] tried to enhance the ASD prediction by using the optimal feature (genes) subsets in the classification algorithm. They used genetic algorithms (GA) and RF in the role of final gene selection. The most important genes selected by each method was used as the input features to the SVM and RF classifiers, cooperating in an ensemble. The final result of the classification was generated by RF and was about 87%.

Chen et al. [32] used the brain images dataset that contains 126 ASD samples and 126 typically developing (TD) samples to detect ASD. Three ML algorithms were implemented in this study to perform a binary classification (ASD vs. TD) using rsfMRI data. First, they used SVM in combination with particle swarm optimization (PSO) for feature selection (PSO-SVM). Second, SVM with recursive feature elimination (RFE-SVM) was used, and thirdly was RF. The diagnostic classification obtained a high accuracy of 91% with RF.

3.2. ASD Prediction Using DL Approach

This study by Noura Samy et al. [27] proposed the IG/DBN model to diagnose ASD. They used DBN based on a Gaussian–Bernoulli Restricted Boltzmann Machine (GBRBM) as a classifier that employs deep learning for ASD classification. The IG filter was used as a gene selector to remove irrelevant genes, and to select the most relevant genes. They used a GE dataset that contains 30 samples and 43,931 features. The proposed model obtained a high accuracy of 98.64%.

Rajat et al. [33] used the published ABIDE dataset, which includes a collection of structural (T1w) and functional (rsfMRI) brain images aggregated across 29 institutions. It includes 1028 participants diagnosed with autism. They explored various transformations that retain the maximum spatial resolution by summarizing the temporal dimension of the rsfMRI data, thus enabling the creation of a full three-dimensional convolutional neural network (3D-CNN) on the ABIDE dataset. They also used the SVM algorithm on the same data set and obtained the highest efficiency at 63%.

Nicha et al. [34] tested six different neural network methods for incorporating phenotypic data such as gender and age, with rsfMRI to classify ASD. They tested the proposed models by using ABIDE. The best model was combining the baseline model directly with raw phenotypic data, and 70.1% accuracy was achieved for ASD classification.

From Table 1, it has been noticed that most of the previous studies applied ML classifiers without using any FS algorithms to build ASD predictive models. Some of these models achieved good result. In addition, there are five studies that have used simple FS with ML algorithms on two data types (PBC and MRI images) [25–29], and the MRI image-based models failed to achieve a high performance compared to the PBC data type. On the other hand, there was limited research on optimizing FS methods using bio-inspired evolutionary algorithms to improve ASD prediction in the literature. Some of these algorithms achieved good results, as follows:

Binary Firefly improved the accuracy to reach 97.9% in [3] with 10 selected features out of 21. GBPSO enhanced the accuracy percentage to 92.1% in [30] with 200 selected features out of 9454. PSO also enhanced the accuracy to reach 91% on an MRI image dataset [32].

From the aforementioned previous studies, we noticed the following:

1. Two methods used for predicting ASD: ML and DL.
2. Multiple ASD datasets such PBC, GE, and IMR brain images are widely used for ASD diagnosis.
3. The 10-fold cross-validation was the most used for dataset partitioning.
4. Bio-inspired algorithms proved their ability to enhance ASD prediction in three types of datasets.
5. MRI brain datasets, compared with the two other datasets types, did not show a high performance in ASD prediction when using ML or DL approaches.

The investigation of optimized feature selection methods using bio-inspired algorithms is limited in the existing ASD research and it has not been well addressed so far in this field. GA [31], PSO [30], and Firefly [3] were the only three bio-inspired algorithms that examined ASD prediction. Over the past few years, there have been some new bio-inspired algorithms that have been developed and used to improve feature selection to solve the high dimensionality problem, especially for disease prediction such as cancer. There are a lot of studies that handled cancer prediction using gene expression profiles and bio-inspired algorithms with ML, such as the bat algorithm (BA), flower pollination algorithm (FPA), grey wolf optimization (GWO), and artificial bee colony (ABC). In [35], a new model was built to predict prostate cancer by using BA with KNN, and it reached a high accuracy 100% and the selected features (genes) were 6 from 500. In [14], GWO with a DT classifier was used to predict Leukemia cancer, they it 100% accuracy. In [36], ABC with NB classification was used to predict Leukemia cancer, which reached 98.68% accuracy with 12 selected features (genes). FPA with SVM was used for breast cancer classification using GE data, and the result was 80.11% accuracy [16].

Therefore, in this study, we aimed to conduct a comparative study and evaluate different bio-inspired-based feature selection algorithms (BA, FPA, GWO, and ABC), which have not been previously applied to ASD prediction, using four ML classifiers (NB, KNN, SVM, and DT), as they are the most widely used algorithms in the literature and showed a good performance in ASD classification on both PBC and GE datasets. To the best of our knowledge, this is the first work to investigate and perform a comparative study on different bio-inspired-based feature selection algorithms for early ASD prediction using PBC and GE datasets.

As the used PBC dataset has been already used in previous work by Vaishali et al. [3] with ML classifiers (NB, KNN, and SVM) and the GE dataset has been used by Noura Samy et al. [27] with ML classifiers (NB, DT, and KNN) and DBN that gave good accuracy results, we used the same classifiers (NB, KNN, SVM, and DT) combined with the proposed optimized wrapper feature selection methods based on GWO, FPA, BA, and ABC for comparison purposes.

4. Materials and Methods

4.1. Anaconda Environment

Anaconda [37] is a simple, open-source platform that helps data scientists interpret their datasets and discover hidden patterns through a number of sophisticated libraries. It is written in the Python language. It is also supported by Linux, MacOS, and Microsoft Windows operating systems and can use Python and R programming languages. In this work, we used Python. Anaconda provides different platforms, which all have specific features. The Jupyter notebook is an interactive notebook computing environment and was used in this project. In addition, the main Python libraries, including NumPy, Pandas, and Scikitlearn, were used.

4.2. Dataset Overview

4.2.1. PBC Dataset

We have obtained the publicly published PBC dataset from UCI (University of California, Irvine), which was compiled by Dr. Fadi Fayez [38]. The data were collected from many countries throughout the world through surveys on a mobile application called "ASD Tests", which can be found in [39]. The data were collected in accordance with the relevant guidelines and regulations. The PBC dataset consists of 292 samples and 20 features used for our training process, and the "class name" feature was used for storing the ASD diagnosis result. The ten features numbered from 11 to 20 were related to personal information, and the other ten features from 1 to 10 consisted of screening questions related to behavior.

4.2.2. GE Dataset

The used GE dataset is publicly available on the National Center for Biotechnology Information (NCBI) [40] and is collected in accordance with the relevant guidelines and regulations. It represents gene expression data for 30 samples with 43,931 features (genes). Classes are divided into 15 ASD and 15 non-ASD.

4.3. Data Preprocessing

4.3.1. PBC Dataset

Data preprocessing entails several steps for the PBC dataset. In order to apply ML algorithms that process the numeric data type, we had to apply the numeric transformation rule to preprocess the four personal string attributes, "gender", "ethnicity", "country of residence", and "who is completing the test", and three binary attributes (with the yes/no answer), "born with jaundice", and "family member with pervasive developmental disorder (PDD)". The attributes of the screening questions were not altered by this rule, as the values were 0 and 1.

4.3.2. GE Dataset

In the GE dataset, we switched the columns and rows as the original dataset was laid out in the opposite way: the attributes were displayed in rows and instances in columns. This step is important as the Pandas library in the Anaconda platform deals with data row by row, where each row represents one sample information.

4.4. Proposed Predictive Models

According to [3], the dimensionality of the used datasets was high (43,931 genes in the GE dataset and 20 features in the PBC) and this may affect the achievement of the classification algorithms. The goal of this work is to enhance the performance of the ML prediction models in terms of accuracy. This goal can be achieved by optimizing the feature selection method using different bio-inspired algorithms.

In this work, we used four bio-inspired algorithms (grey wolf optimizer, flower pollination algorithm, bat algorithm, and artificial bee colony) with four ML classifiers (NB, KNN, DT, and SVM). To our knowledge, these four bio-inspired algorithms have not yet been examined for ASD classification. As we mentioned previously in the related work, we tried to investigate and compare the performance of two bio-inspired optimization algorithms (FPA and GWO) that are considered newer than two well-known algorithms (BA and ABC), which have proven their ability to enhance diseases classification such as cancer when dealing with a high dimensionality dataset like GE. These algorithms are compared in terms of search efficiency and robustness for finding the optimal feature subset for the classification process.

Therefore, we developed 16 optimized predictive models as follows: GWO-NB, GWO-KNN, GWO-SVM, GWO-DT, FPA-NB, FPA-KNN, FPA-SVM, FPA-DT, BA-NB, BA-KNN, BA-SVM, BA-DT, ABC-NB, ABC-KNN, ABC-SVM, and ABC-DT. Figure 2 presents the general framework of the proposed model.

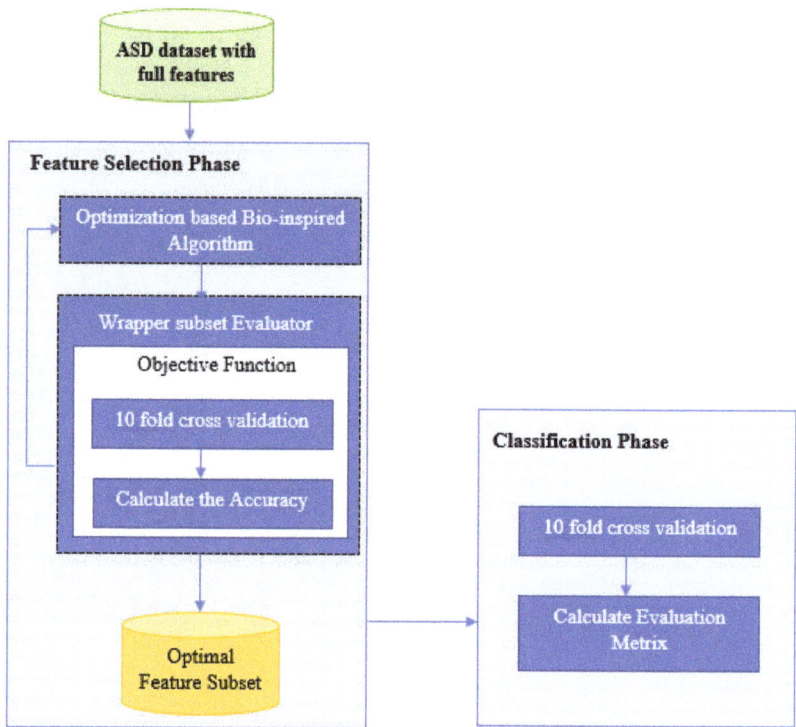

Figure 2. The general framework of the proposed models.

As illustrated in Figure 2, the main framework of the proposed model consisted of two main phases: the feature selection phase and the classification phase.

4.4.1. The Feature Selection Phase

In the beginning, we used the wrapper selection method for feature selection, and we optimized its performance by incorporating it into it the bio-inspired algorithms (GWO, BA, FPA, and ABC). This phase starts with a population of the candidate solutions (PBC or GE features). Next, the candidate solutions were evaluated using objective function (wrapper subset evaluator). The objective function aims to evaluate each solution according to the used fitness function, which depends on the ML classifier (SVM in our case) in order to get the classification accuracy of each solution. Therefore, from the candidate solutions, the solutions with the highest accuracy were selected as the optimal feature subset. The resulting optimal feature subset in this phase was used in the second phase, which is the classification phase. The main parameter settings that were used in this work of the four wrapper methods were the number of solutions (N) = 10 and the number of iterations (i) = 20.

4.4.2. The Classification Phase

The final optimal features, which were the output of the first phase will be used to evaluate the classifiers. In this phase, the classifier was trained using the training dataset with optimal features, and the testing dataset was employed to test the performance of the classifier. This work adopted the 10-fold cross-validation, and the final classification was made based on the average. The classification results were evaluated using the five evaluation metric. In this research, the LinearSVC (C = 1) from sklearn library was applied for performance evaluation in both objective function and final classification that used SVM.

For the NB classification algorithm we used the GaussianNB from sklearn library for the evaluation and analysis. For the NB classifier, we used the GaussianNB from sklearn library and we adopted the KNeighborsClassifier (k = 5), and we utilized the DecisionTreeClassifier with an entropy value from the sklearn library for evaluating the performance.

5. Implementation and Results

In this work we conducted three experiments. In the first experiment, we applied the four predictive classifiers (NB, KNN, SVM, and DT) without using the optimized wrapper selection method for the sake of comparison. In the second experiment, we evaluated the performance of the 16 proposed models and compared the obtained results with the first experiment and previous works [3,27]. In the third experiment, we employed the CNN deep learning approach to compare its results with the proposed models.

5.1. Experiment 1

For the sake of comparison and to investigate the advantage of using the optimized wrapper selection methods based on bio-inspired algorithms, we conducted the first experiment in which we used the four classical ML classifiers (NB, KNN, SVM, and DT) with the two datasets (PBC and GE) for ASD prediction without using the optimized wrapper selection method.

Table 5 presents the results of the four classifiers on the two datasets. As we can see from the table, the DT classifier achieved the highest accuracy with the PBC dataset. For the GE dataset, we noticed that the highest accuracy was 86.6% obtained by DT.

Table 5. First Experiment Results.

Data Type	PBC					GE				
Eva. Metrix	Acc	F1-Score	Precision	Recall	AUC	Acc	F1-Score	Precision	Recall	AUC
NB	93.49	93.0	94.0	93.0	93.52	66.7	64.0	73.0	67.0	67.0
KNN	89.03	89.0	89.0	89.0	90.0	56.66	57.0	77.0	57.0	59.9
SVM	91.7	92.0	92.0	92.0	92.2	80.0	80.0	82.0	80.0	80.3
DT	95.5	96.0	96.0	96.0	95.9	86.6	87.0	87.0	87.0	88.1

Therefore, we can see that using ML classifiers without any FS methods for the GE dataset did not give an efficient ASD prediction compared to the PBC dataset due to its high dimensionality. It has also been noticed that the accuracy of KNN was relatively low, especially when compared to other classification algorithms for all datasets.

5.2. Experiment 2

In this experiment, we investigated the impact of incorporating the optimized wrapper feature selection method based on the bio-inspired algorithms (GWO, FPA, BA, and ABC) into the used predictive classifiers (NB, KNN, SVM, and DT) using two datasets (PBC and GE). Table 6 presents the obtained results of the proposed models.

Regarding the PBC dataset, Figure 3 shows the obtained accuracy results for the proposed models. It can be seen from Table 6 and Figure 3 that the GWO-SVM and GWO-DT models gave the highest accuracy results of 99.66% and 98.29%, respectively, compared to the GWO-NB model (97.58%), followed by the GWO-KNN model (96.89%). The FPA-SVM model achieved the highest accuracy of 99.56% compared with the FPA-DT model (96.21%) and the FPA-KNN (95.52%), while the lowest accuracy was obtained by the FPA-NB model (94.88%). On the other hand, the BA-based wrapper models gave the highest accuracy with the BA-SVM (98.97%) and BA-NB models (97.60%) compared to the BA-DT model (96.22%), followed by the BA-KNN model (93.14%). For ABC-based wrapper models, the ABC-SVM model gave the highest accuracy (98.63%) compared with the ABC-KNN model (98.27%) and the ABC-DT (97.73%). The ABC-NB model gave the lowest accuracy of 95.54%. According to the obtained results, GWO-SVM had the best classification performance on the PBC dataset compared to the remaining classifiers.

Table 6. Second Experiment Results.

Data Type	PBC					GE				
	Grey Wolf Optimization									
	AUC	Recall	Precision	F1-Score	Acc	AUC	Recall	Precision	F1-Score	Acc
NB	97.58	97.48	97.89	97.14	97.57	63.34	43.0	46.66	45.0	60.0
KNN	96.89	96.79	97.23	96.42	96.88	63.33	72.0	58.33	100	62.5
SVM	99.66	99.67	99.33	100	99.69	99.34	96.0	100	92.66	99.33
DT	98.29	98.16	98.54	97.85	98.27	80.0	83.33	81.66	95.0	85.0
	Flower Pollination Algorithm									
NB	94.88	94.61	94.56	95.04	94.87	70.0	59.66	61.66	60.0	61.0
KNN	95.52	95.33	95.10	95.76	95.54	60.0	70.33	56.66	100	60.0
SVM	99.56	99.65	99.33	100	99.66	96.67	97.14	95.0	100	96.67
DT	96.21	95.98	97.10	95.0	96.16	76.66	69.33	68.33	75.0	72.5
	Bat Algorithm									
NB	97.60	97.50	98.61	96.47	97.57	63.33	43.33	50.0	40.0	57.5
KNN	93.14	92.82	93.63	92.85	93.09	56.66	68.33	53.33	100	55.0
SVM	98.97	98.78	98.01	100	99.0	97.43	97.33	97.33	97.33	97.34
DT	96.22	95.83	97.75	94.22	96.11	89.99	91.66	93.33	95.0	92.0
	Artificial Bee Colony									
NB	95.54	95.02	97.90	92.85	95.42	56.66	48.33	55.0	45.0	52.5
KNN	98.27	98.22	97.90	98.57	98.28	53.33	66.67	51.66	100	52.5
SVM	98.63	98.61	98.08	99.28	98.66	96.66	96.0	100	93.33	96.67
DT	97.73	97.89	98.06	97.85	97.92	93.33	94.66	91.66	100	92.5

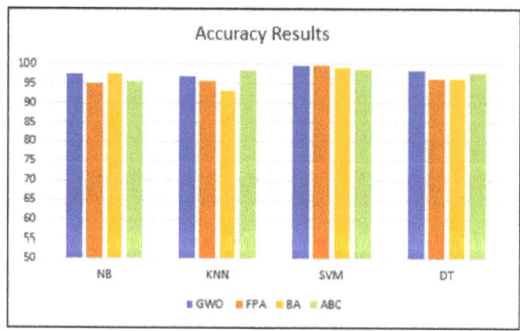

Figure 3. Comparison of accuracy between proposed models on PBC dataset.

Regarding the GE dataset, Figure 4 shows the accuracy results of the proposed models. GWO-SVM had the highest accuracy of 99.34% compared to the GWO-DT model (80.0%), followed by the GWO-KNN (63.34%) and GWO-NB models (63.33%). As for the FPA-based models, the FPA-SVM model gave the highest accuracy (96.67%) compared with the FPA-DT model (76.66%) and the FPA-NB (70.0%). The FPA-KNN model had the lowest accuracy of 60.0%. On the other hand, the BA-based models gave the highest accuracy with the SVM-BA model (97.34%) compared to the BA-DT model (89.99%), followed by the BA-NB model (63.33%), and BA-KNN gave the lowest accuracy of 56.66%. For ABC-based models, the ABC-SVM model gave the highest accuracy (96.66%) compared with the ABC-DT model (93.33%) and ABC-NB (56.66%), while the lowest accuracy was 53.33% for the ABC-KNN model.

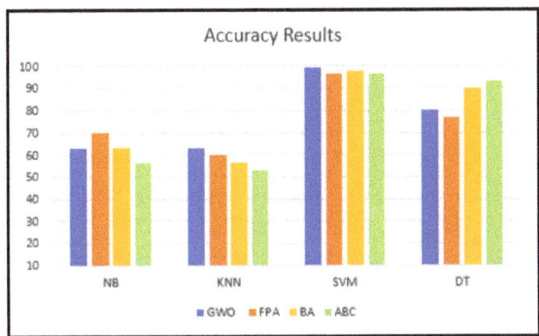

Figure 4. Comparison of accuracy between proposed models on the GE dataset.

According to the obtained results, GWO-SVM had the best classification performance on the GE dataset compared to the remaining classifiers. In general, we can say that the proposed models achieved a good predictive performance on the two datasets. For the PBC dataset, the SVM and DT classifiers had a better performance with the four optimized wrapper methods. GWO-SVM and FPA-SVM were the best models with highest accuracies of 99.66% and 99.56%, respectively. As for the GE dataset, the SVM classifier was better with the four optimized wrapper methods than the other classifiers. GWO-SVM and BA-SVM were the best models with the highest accuracies of 99.34% and 97.43%, respectively.

Figure 5 presents the F1 score results of the 16 proposed models on PBC dataset. The SVM classifier gave the highest results with the GWO, FPA, BA, and ABC-based models (99.67%, 99.65%, 98.78%, and 98.61%, respectively) compared to the other classifiers. On the other hand, the BA-KNN model gave the lowest result (92.82%).

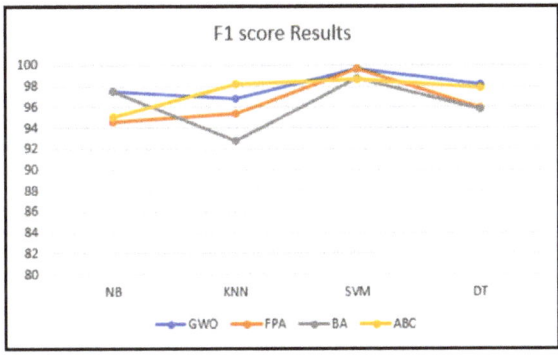

Figure 5. Comparison of F1 score results between proposed models on PBC dataset.

Figure 6 presents the F1 score results of the 16 proposed models on the GE dataset. The SVM classifier gave the highest results with GWO, FPA, BA, and ABC-based models (96.0%, 97.14%, 97.33%, and 96.0%, respectively) compared to the other classifiers. On the other hand, the BA-NB model gave the lowest result (43.33%).

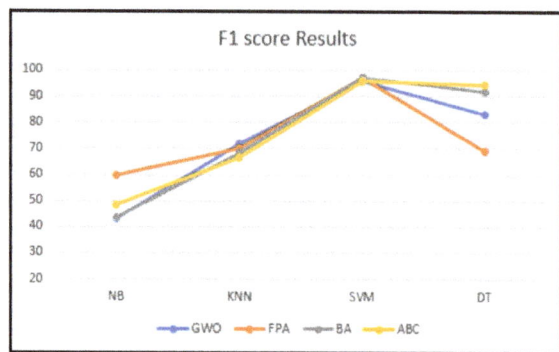

Figure 6. Comparison of F1 score results between proposed models on the GE dataset.

Figure 7 shows the graphical representation of the ROC curves for all four classifiers in each wrapper selection method on the PBC dataset. In the ROC curves of the GWO-based wrapper models the SVM curve covers more areas, followed by DT and then NB and KNN (99.69%, 98.27%, 97.57%, and 96.88%, respectively). In the ROC curves of the FPA-based wrapper models, the SVM curve covered more areas, followed by DT and then KNN and NB (99.66%, 96.16%, 95.54%, and 94.87%, respectively). In the ROC curves of BA-based wrapper models the SVM curve covers more areas, followed by the NB and then the DT and KNN (99.0%, 97.57%, 96.11%, and 93.09%, respectively). In the ROC curves of ABC-based wrapper models the SVM curve covers more areas, followed by the KNN and then the DT and NB (98.66%, 98.28%, 97.92%, and 95.42%, respectively).

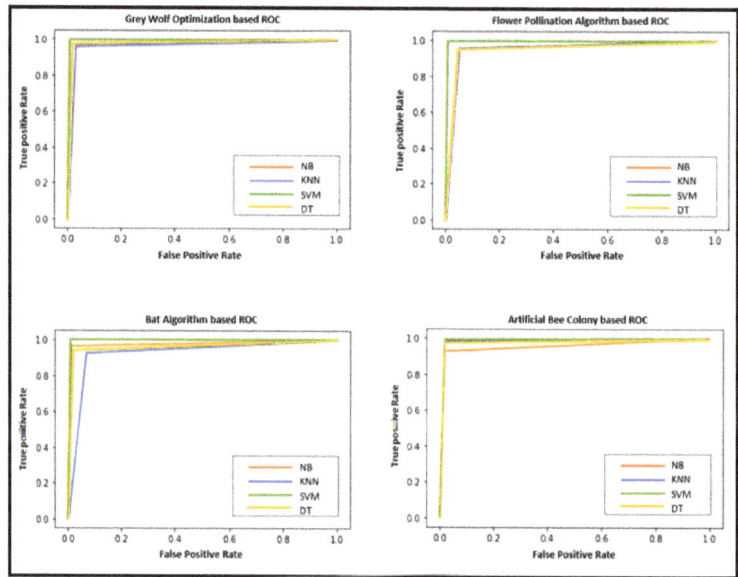

Figure 7. ROC curves of the proposed models on the GE dataset.

Figure 8 shows the AUC results for all four classifiers in each wrapper selection method in the GE dataset. In the ROC curves of the GWO-based wrapper models, the SVM curve covers more areas, followed by DT, and then KNN and NB (99.33%, 85.0%, 62.5%, and 60.0%, respectively). In the ROC curves of FPA-based wrapper models, the SVM curve covered more areas, followed by DT, and then NB and KNN (96.67%, 72.5%, 61.0%, and 60.0%, respectively). In the ROC curves of the BA-based wrapper models, the SVM curve covered more areas, followed by DT, and then NB and KNN (97.34%, 92.0%, 57.5%, and 55.0%, respectively) In the ROC curves of the ABC-based wrapper models the SVM curve covers more areas, followed by KNN, and then DT and NB (96.67%, 96.67%, 52.5%, and 52.5%, respectively).

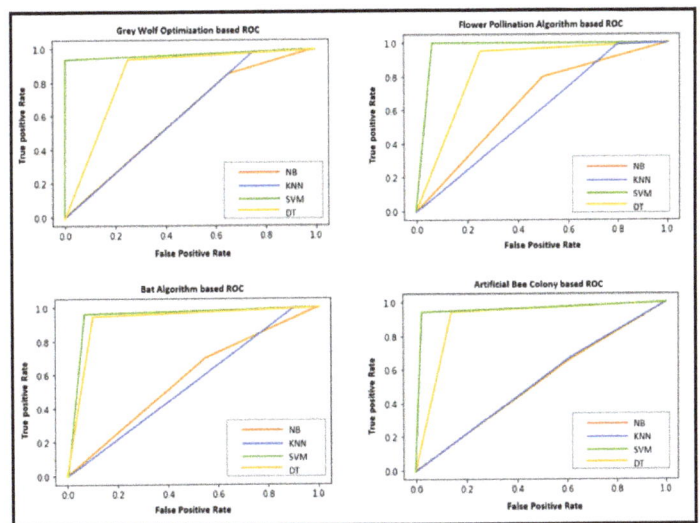

Figure 8. ROC curves of the proposed models on the PBC dataset.

The precision results in the PBC dataset were the best in GWO-SVM and FPA-SVM, while GWO-SVM and ABC-SVM returned the best results in the GE dataset. Moreover, GWO-SVM and BA-SVM gave the best recall results in the PBC dataset, while GWO-KNN, FPA-KNN, FPA-SVM, BA-KNN, and ABC-KNN returned the best results in the GE dataset with 100%.

Furthermore, Table 7 shows the number of selected features in each model for two datasets. For the PBC dataset, the BA-based wrapper model obtained the minimum number of features compared to the other models. For the GE dataset, the GWO-based wrapper model obtained the minimum number of genes compared to other models. Therefore, this was reflected in the ability of the GWO-SVM, FPA-SVM, BA-SVM, and ABC-SVM models to gain the highest accuracy results. In general, all algorithms succeeded in reducing the high dimensionality of our datasets.

Table 7. Final optimal features.

Data Type	Before Optimized FS	After Optimized FS			
		Algorithm			
		GWO	FPA	BA	ABC
PBC	20	6	13	4	12
GE	43,931	15,392	21,714	21,556	21,469

5.2.1. Comparison between Experiment 1 and Experiment 2

In this section, we compare the results of the first experiment, which used all of the features of the datasets along with Experiment 2, which selected the most informative subset of the features using the proposed wrapper selection method.

According to Figures 9 and 10, and Tables 6 and 7, we observed the following: From Figure 9, we can see that all classifiers' accuracies were enhanced after using the GWO, FPA, BA, and ABC-based wrapper methods. The best model that obtained the best accuracy on the PBC dataset was GWO-SVM (99.66%) in Experiment 2, while the DT classifier gave the highest accuracy of 95.5% in Experiment 1.

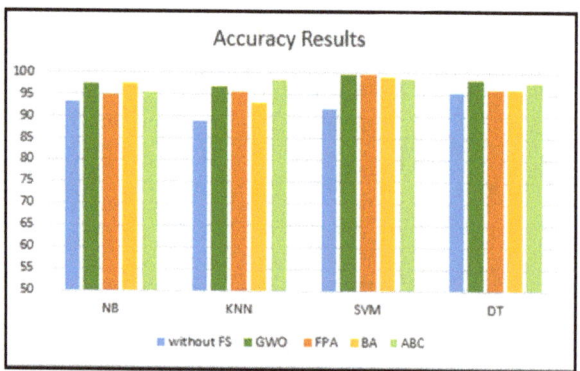

Figure 9. Comparison of accuracy between Experiment 1 and Experiment 2 on the PBC dataset.

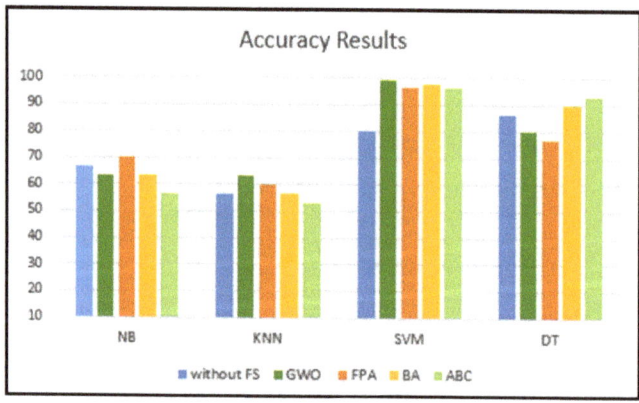

Figure 10. Comparison of accuracy between Experiment 1 and Experiment 2 on GE dataset.

On other hand, Figure 10 shows that all classifiers' accuracies were enhanced after using the GWO, FPA, BA, and ABC-based wrapper methods on the GE dataset. The best accuracy achieved in Experiment 2 was 99.34% for GWO-SVM, while the best accuracy obtained in Experiment 1 was 86.6% for the DT classifier.

Moreover, the size of the features was reduced to 6 after using GWO for the PBC dataset and 15,392 for the GE dataset. Regarding AUC, F1score, precision, and recall, they were also enhanced after using the GWO, FPA, BA, and ABC-based wrapper selection methods for the two datasets.

5.2.2. Comparison between the Proposed Models and Previous Work

In this part, we compare the results of the previous work in the literature, which used the Firefly feature selection algorithm with SVM classifier (FA-SVM) on the PBC dataset [3] and IG filter with a deep belief network algorithm for classification (DBN-IG) on the GE dataset [27], with the four best obtained results of the proposed models, which selected the most informative subset of features.

According to results for the PBC dataset from Tables 7 and 8, we observed that the four proposed models gave better accuracy of results compared with previous work [3], and the GWO-SVM model had the highest accuracy with 99.66%. Moreover, the size of the features in the proposed models was reduced to 4 by the BA-based wrapper model and 6 by the GWO-based wrapper model, rather than 10 by FA-based wrapper model [3]. Based on the results of the GE dataset from Tables 7 and 9, we observed that the GWO-SVM proposed model enhanced the accuracy to 99.34% compared with the accuracy of the previous work [27], which was 98.64%.

Table 8. Comparison between the proposed models and previous work [3] on the PBC dataset.

	Previous Work [3]	Proposed Models			
	FA-SVM	GWO-SVM	FPA-SVM	BA-SVM	ABC-SVM
Accuracy	97.95%	99.66%	99.5%	98.9%	98.63%

Table 9. Comparison between the proposed models and previous work [27] on the GE dataset.

	Previous Work [27]	Proposed Models			
	DBN-IG	GWO-SVM	FPA-SVM	BA-SVM	ABC-SVM
Accuracy	98.64%	99.34%	96.6%	97.4%	96.66%

To sum up, the experimental results showed the effectiveness of incorporating the optimized wrapper feature selection based on bio-inspired algorithms (GWO, FPA, BA, and ABC) into the four predictive classifiers (NB, KNN, SVM, and DT) in terms of the accuracy of ASD prediction for the PBC dataset and GE dataset.

5.2.3. Comparison between the Proposed Models and the DL Based Model

In this section, we compared the highest results of the 16 proposed models with the CNN model that was employed for ASD classification. According to the obtained results, for the PBC dataset from Table 10, we observed that the GWO-SVM gave better accuracy results of 99.66% compared to the CNN model (98.64). This can be attributed to the small size of the PBC dataset.

Table 10. Comparison between the proposed models and the DL-based model.

	PBC		GE	
	CNN	GWO-SVM	CNN	GWO-SVM
Accuracy	98.64%	99.66%	99.98%	99.34%

Based on the results of the GE dataset from Table 10, we observed that the CNN model achieved better accuracy of 99.98% compared to the accuracy obtained by GWO-SVM, which was 99.34%.

6. Conclusions and Future Work

Several different ML algorithms that can be used for ASD detection; however, some of them are unnecessarily time-consuming and prone to human error, and thus by the time the disease is detected, the patient may already be in the stage of ASD that is difficult to deal with. The challenge is to implement an automatic, fast, and accurate model for early ASD detection.

This project aims to assess the ability of optimizing the wrapper FS method based on bio-inspired algorithms (GWO, FPA, BA, and ABC) to enhance the prediction accuracy of 16 ML models (GWO-NB, GWO-KNN, GWO-SVM, GWO-DT, FPA-NB, FPA-KNN, FPA-SVM,

FPA-DT, BA-NB, BA-KNN, BA-SVM, BA-DT, ABC-NB, ABC-KNN, ABC-SVM, and ABC-DT). The optimized wrapper FS methods were thus implemented with four different ML classifiers, NB, KNN, SVM, and DT. All of the algorithms were evaluated on two datasets and were compared with the results for the original classifiers.

The experimental results showed the effectiveness of the proposed models in terms of the prediction accuracy of ASD, especially when we used the GE dataset. Generally, the models produced a good accuracy with both the PBC and GE datasets. Among all 16 models, GWO-SVM obtained the highest accuracy overall for both the PBC and GE datasets. In addition, the DL-based model achieved better accuracy results with big datasets such as GE rather than the PBC dataset. The main limitations faced in this work were the significant computation time when the number of features was large, as well as the large amount of memory and more powerful processor.

In the future, the aim is to compare these algorithms based on bio-inspired algorithms with deep learning approaches for ASD prediction after obtaining more patient samples. Moreover, the combination between two dataset types with the same samples may provide more accurate results. Hybrid feature selection may also be used as a future approach, as it combines the advantages of both filter and wrapper algorithms.

Author Contributions: M.A. developed the model and performed the experiments. H.H.A.-B. verified the analytical methods. All authors conceived the study and H.H.A.-B. was in charge of overall direction and planning. All authors have read and agreed to the published version of the manuscript.

Funding: This research received no external funding.

Informed Consent Statement: Not Applicable.

Data Availability Statement: The two analyzed datasets during the current study are publicly published. The GE dataset is available in the National Center for Biotechnology Information (NCBI) repository, https://www.ncbi.nlm.nih.gov/ (accessed on 7 March 2022), and the PBC dataset is available in the Center for Machine Learning and Intelligent Systems repository, https://archive.ics.uci.edu/ (accessed on 7 March 2022).

Acknowledgments: The authors would like to acknowledge the Researchers Supporting Project Number (RSP-2021/287), King Saud University, Riyadh, Saudi Arabia for their support in this work.

Conflicts of Interest: The authors declare no conflict of interest.

Abbreviations

Abbreviation	Definition
ASD	Autism spectrum disorder
ML	Machine learning
DL	Deep learning
GE	Gene expression
PBC	Personal and behavioral characteristics
GWO	Gray wolf optimization
FPA	Flower pollination algorithm
BA	Bat algorithms
ABC	Artificial bee colony
AUC	Area under the curve
SVM	Support vector machine
DT	Decision tree
NB	Naïve Bayes
KNN	K-nearest neighbor
FS	Feature selection
NIC	Nature-inspired computation
UCI	University of California, Irvine
LR	Linear regression
LDA	Linear discriminant analysis

RF	Random forest
SVC	Support vector classifier
RT	Random tree
CFS	Correlation feature selection
BT	Bagged tree feature selector
REF	Recursive feature elimination
IG	Information gain
SMO	Sequential minimal optimization
ABIDE	Autism brain imaging data exchange dataset
GBM	Gradient boosting machine
GBPSO	Geometric binary particle swarm optimization
WRS	Wilcoxon rank sum test
PSO	Particle swarm optimization
RFE	Recursive feature elimination
PDD	Pervasive developmental disorder

References

1. Hirvikoski, T.; Mittendorfer-Rutz, E.; Boman, M.; Larsson, H.; Lichtenstein, P.; Bölte, S. Premature mortality in autism spectrum disorder. *Br. J. Psychiatry* **2016**, *208*, 232–238. [CrossRef] [PubMed]
2. Bolón-Canedo, V.; Sánchez-Maroño, N.; Alonso-Betanzos, A. Feature selection for high-dimensional data. *Prog. Artif. Intell.* **2016**, *5*, 65–75. [CrossRef]
3. Vaishali, R.; Sasikala, R. A machine learning based approach to classify autism with optimum behavior sets. *Int. J. Eng. Technol.* **2018**, *7*, 1–6. [CrossRef]
4. Al-Baity, H.H.; Al-Mutlaq, N. A New Optimized Wrapper Gene Selection Method for Breast Cancer Prediction. *Comput. Mater. Contin.* **2021**, *67*, 3089–3106. [CrossRef]
5. Erkan, U.; Thanh, D. Autism Spectrum Disorder Detection with Machine Learning Methods. *Curr. Psychiatry Rev.* **2019**, *15*, 297–308. [CrossRef]
6. Raza, K. *Analysis of Microarray Data Using Artificial Intelligence Based Techniques*; IGI Global: Hershey, PA, USA, 2016; pp. 216–239.
7. Suthaharan, S. *Machine Learning Models and Algorithms for Big Data Classification: Thinking with Examples for Effective Learning*; Springer: New York, NY, USA, 2015; p. 36.
8. Almugren, N.; Alshamlan, H. A Survey on Hybrid Feature Selection Methods in Microarray Gene Expression Data for Cancer Classification. *IEEE Access* **2019**, *7*, 78533–78548. [CrossRef]
9. Li, J.; Cheng, K.; Wang, S.; Morstatter, F.; Trevino, R.P.; Tang, J.; Liu, H. Feature Selection: A Data Perspective. *ACM Comput. Surv.* **2017**, *50*, 94:1–94:45. [CrossRef]
10. Lazar, C.; Taminau, J.; Meganck, S.; Steenhoff, D.; Coletta, A.; Molter, C.; de Schaetzen, V.; Duque, R.; Bersini, H.; Nowe, A. A survey on filter techniques for feature selection in gene expression microarray analysis. *IEEE/ACM Trans. Comput. Biol. Bioinform.* **2012**, *9*, 1106–1119. [CrossRef]
11. Sheikhpour, R.; Sarram, M.A.; Sheikhpour, R. Particle swarm optimization for bandwidth determination and feature selection of kernel density estimation based classifiers in diagnosis of breast cancer. *Appl. Soft Comput.* **2016**, *40*, 113–131. [CrossRef]
12. Fan, X.; Sayers, W.; Zhang, S.; Han, Z.; Ren, L.; Chizari, H. Review and Classification of Bio-inspired Algorithms and Their Applications. *J. Bionic Eng.* **2020**, *17*, 611–631. [CrossRef]
13. Fister, I., Jr.; Yang, X.-S.; Fister, I.; Brest, J.; Fister, D. A Brief Review of Nature-Inspired Algorithms for Optimization. *Elektrotehniski Vestn./Electrotech. Rev.* **2013**, *80*, 116–122.
14. Applying Grey Wolf Optimizer-Based Decision Tree Classifer for Cancer Classification on Gene Expression Data | IEEE Conference Publication | IEEE Xplore. Available online: https://ieeexplore.ieee.org/document/7365818 (accessed on 17 April 2021).
15. Yang, X.-S. A New Metaheuristic Bat-Inspired Algorithm. In *Nature Inspired Cooperative Strategies for Optimization (NICSO 2010)*; González, J.R.; Pelta, D.A.; Cruz, C.; Terrazas, G.; Krasnogor, N., Eds.; Springer: Berlin/Heidelberg, Germany, 2010; pp. 65–74.
16. Dankolo, N.; Radzi, N.; Sallehuddin, R.; Mustaffa, N. Hybrid Flower Pollination Algorithm and Support Vector Machine for Breast Cancer Classification. *J. Technol. Manag. Bus.* **2018**, *5*, 1. [CrossRef]
17. A Simple and Efficient Artificial Bee Colony Algorithm. *Math. Probl. Eng.* **2013**, *2013*, 526315. Available online: https://www.hindawi.com/jour-nals/mpe/2013/526315/ (accessed on 3 December 2020).
18. Tyagi, B.; Mishra, R.; Bajpai, N. Machine Learning Techniques to Predict Autism Spectrum Disorder. In Proceedings of the 2018 IEEE Punecon, Pune, India, 30 November–2 December 2018; pp. 1–5. [CrossRef]
19. Chinnaiyan, R. Optimized Machine Learning Classification Approaches for Prediction of Autism Spectrum Disorder. *Ann. Autism. Dev. Disord.* **2020**, *1*, 1–6.
20. ALARIFI, H.S.; YOUNG, G.S. Using multiple machine learning algorithms to predict autism in children. In Proceedings of the International Conference on Artificial Intelligence (ICAI). The Steering Committee of The World Congress in Computer Science, Computer Engineering and Applied Computing (WorldComp), Las Vegas, NV, USA, 30 July–2 August 2018; pp. 464–467.

21. Oh, D.H.; Kim, I.B.; Kim, S.H.; Ahn, D.H. Predicting Autism Spectrum Disorder Using Blood-based Gene Expression Signatures and Machine Learning. *Clin. Psychopharmacol. Neurosci.* **2017**, *15*, 47–52. [CrossRef]
22. Sudha, V.P.; Vijaya, M.S. Machine Learning-Based Model for Identification of Syndromic Autism Spectrum Disorder. In *Integrated Intelligent Computing, Communication and Security*; Krishna, A.N., Srikantaiah, K.C., Naveena, C., Eds.; Springer: Singapore, 2019; Volume 771, pp. 141–148.
23. Asif, M.; Martiniano, H.F.M.C.M.; Vicente, A.M.; Couto, F.M. Identifying disease genes using machine learning and gene functional similarities, assessed through Gene Ontology. *PLoS ONE* **2018**, *13*, e0208626. [CrossRef]
24. Katuwal, G.J.; Cahill, N.D.; Baum, S.A.; Michael, A.M. The predictive power of structural MRI in Autism diagnosis. In Proceedings of the 2015 37th Annual International Conference of the IEEE Engineering in Medicine and Biology Society (EMBC), Milan, Italy, 25–29 August 2015; pp. 4270–4273. [CrossRef]
25. Selvaraj, S.; Palanisamy, P.; Parveen, S. Monisha. Autism Spectrum Disorder Prediction Using Machine Learning Algorithms. In *Computational Vision and Bio-Inspired Computing*; Smys, S., Tavares, J.M.R.S., Balas, V.E., Iliyasu, A.M., Eds.; Springer International Publishing: Cham, Switzerland, 2020; Volume 1108, pp. 496–503.
26. Hossain, M.D.; Kabir, M.A.; Anwar, A.; Islam, M.Z. Detecting Autism Spectrum Disorder using Machine Learning. *arXiv* **2020**, arXiv:2009.14249.
27. Samy, N.; Fathalla, R.; Belal, N.A.; Badawy, O. Classification of Autism Gene Expression Data Using Deep Learning. *Intelligent Data Communication Technologies and Internet of Things* **2019**, 583–596.
28. Jin, Y.; Wee, C.Y.; Shi, F.; Thung, K.H.; Ni, D.; Yap, P.T.; Shen, D. Identification of infants at high-risk for autism spectrum disorder using multiparameter multiscale white matter connectivity networks. *Hum. Brain Mapp.* **2015**, *36*, 4880–4896. [CrossRef]
29. Katuwal, G.J. *Machine Learning Based Autism Detection Using Brain Imaging*; Rochester Institute of Technology: Rochester, NY, USA, 2017.
30. Hameed, S.S.; Hassan, R.; Muhammad, F.F. Selection and classification of gene expression in autism disorder: Use of a combination of statistical filters and a GBPSO-SVM algorithm. *PLoS ONE* **2017**, *12*, e0187371. [CrossRef]
31. Latkowski, T.; Osowski, S. Developing Gene Classifier System for Autism Recognition. In *Advances in Computational Intelligence*; Springer: Cham, Switzerland, 2015; pp. 3–14. [CrossRef]
32. Chen, C.P.; Keown, C.L.; Jahedi, A.; Nair, A.; Pflieger, M.E.; Bailey, B.A.; Müller, R.A. Diagnostic classification of intrinsic functional connectivity highlights somatosensory, default mode, and visual regions in autism. *NeuroImage Clin.* **2015**, *8*, 238–245. [CrossRef] [PubMed]
33. Thomas, R.M.; Gallo, S.; Cerliani, L.; Zhutovsky, P.; El-Gazzar, A.; van Wingen, G. Classifying Autism Spectrum Disorder Using the Temporal Statistics of Resting-State Functional MRI Data With 3D Convolutional Neural Networks. *Front. Psychiatry* **2020**, *11*, 440. [CrossRef] [PubMed]
34. Dvornek, N.C.; Ventola, P.; Duncan, J.S. Combining phenotypic and resting-state fMRI data for autism classification with recurrent neural networks. In Proceedings of the 2018 IEEE 15th International Symposium on Biomedical Imaging (ISBI 2018), Washington, DC, USA, 4–7 April 2018; pp. 725–728. [CrossRef]
35. Dashtban, M.; Balafar, M.; Suravajhala, P. Gene selection for tumor classification using a novel bio-inspired multi-objective approach. *Genomics* **2018**, *110*, 10–17. [CrossRef] [PubMed]
36. Musheer, R.; Verma, C.K.; Srivastava, N. Dimension reduction methods for microarray data: A review. *AIMS Bioeng.* **2017**, *4*, 179–197. [CrossRef]
37. Introduction to Data Science: A Python Approach to Concepts, Techniques and Applications. 2017. Available online: https://www.worldcat.org/title/introduction-to-data-science-a-python-approach-to-concepts-techniques-and-applications/oclc/986740318 (accessed on 17 April 2021).
38. UCI Machine Learning Repository: Autistic Spectrum Disorder Screening Data for Children Data Set. Available online: https://archive.ics.uci.edu/ml/datasets/Autistic+Spectrum+Disorder+Screening+Data+for+Children++ (accessed on 2 December 2020).
39. ASD. Autism Spectrum Disorder Tests App. Available online: http://www.asdtests.com/ (accessed on 2 December 2020).
40. National Center for Biotechnology Information. Available online: https://www.ncbi.nlm.nih.gov/ (accessed on 18 November 2020).

Article

Dog Behavior Recognition Based on Multimodal Data from a Camera and Wearable Device

Jinah Kim and Nammee Moon *

Department of Computer Science and Engineering, Hoseo University, Asan-si 31499, Korea; kkim.jinah00@gmail.com
* Correspondence: nammee.moon@gmail.com

Abstract: Although various studies on monitoring dog behavior have been conducted, methods that can minimize or compensate data noise are required. This paper proposes multimodal data-based dog behavior recognition that fuses video and sensor data using a camera and a wearable device. The video data represent the moving area of dogs to detect the dogs. The sensor data represent the movement of the dogs and extract features that affect dog behavior recognition. Seven types of behavior recognition were conducted, and the results of the two data types were used to recognize the dog's behavior through a fusion model based on deep learning. Experimentation determined that, among FasterRCNN, YOLOv3, and YOLOv4, the object detection rate and behavior recognition accuracy were the highest when YOLOv4 was used. In addition, the sensor data showed the best performance when all statistical features were selected. Finally, it was confirmed that the performance of multimodal data-based fusion models was improved over that of single data-based models and that the CNN-LSTM-based model had the best performance. The method presented in this study can be applied for dog treatment or health monitoring, and it is expected to provide a simple way to estimate the amount of activity.

Keywords: multimodal data; behavior recognition; dog detection; fusion model; deep learning

Citation: Kim, J.; Moon, N. Dog Behavior Recognition Based on Multimodal Data from a Camera and Wearable Device. *Appl. Sci.* **2022**, *12*, 3199. https://doi.org/10.3390/app12063199

Academic Editor: Federico Divina

Received: 15 January 2022
Accepted: 18 March 2022
Published: 21 March 2022

Publisher's Note: MDPI stays neutral with regard to jurisdictional claims in published maps and institutional affiliations.

Copyright: © 2022 by the authors. Licensee MDPI, Basel, Switzerland. This article is an open access article distributed under the terms and conditions of the Creative Commons Attribution (CC BY) license (https:// creativecommons.org/licenses/by/ 4.0/).

1. Introduction

Recently, as the number of families raising pets such as dogs and cats has increased, interest in human–pet interaction (HPI) has also increased. For HPI, it is necessary to know the emotions and health conditions of pets; however, it is difficult for humans to recognize pets' expressions. To solve this issue, monitoring studies of behavioral observation of dogs using cameras, wearable devices, and pet products are being conducted [1–3].

Among them, the basic factor monitored in dogs in daily life is the dog's amount of activity, such as the number of steps it takes. Like a smartwatch worn by a human, a wearable device records how much the wearer has moved. In addition, such devices make it possible to understand the sleeping time or patterns of the dog; when changes in the dog's movement are observed or the amount of activity decreases rapidly, a disease may be suspected.

To determine the activity level of dogs, a video camera or a wearable device can be used. A camera is installed in the house to observe the dog's behavior in an empty house, so it is widely used in monitoring research for disease care [2–4]. For a wearable device, various sensors can be used to analyze a dog's movements. There are various commercial wearable devices such as Petpace, Fitbark, and Whistle, that measure and track the number of steps taken by a dog, which serves as a proxy for activity level [1,5].

With the combination of the technologies of Internet of Things (IoT), machine learning, and artificial intelligence, the amount of activity in dogs can be specified. In the past, only the direction or speed of the movement of the dog in the video was detected, or the activity level was estimated in 3–5 steps with data centered on acceleration for wearable devices.

Recently, the amount of activity has been obtained through recognition of the behavior of dogs. Through examination of the detection area or joint movement in the video or embedding various sensors such as a gyroscope and inertial measurement unit (IMU) in the wearable device, it became possible to recognize specific behaviors such as sitting and standing, which greatly improved the accuracy [1]. With these methods, detailed dog monitoring is possible if the amount of activity is obtained through behavior recognition of dogs. For example, since it is possible to measure the calorie consumption for each behavior, it is possible to suggest an appropriate amount or type of feed. In addition, in the case of a dog whose leg has been operated on, the degree of movement can be checked for rehabilitation, and exercise can be recommended on days when there is little movement.

However, various issues may arise in the process of collecting the behavior data of dogs. Cameras should be installed in such a way that as little overlapping with people or other objects occurs as possible. In addition, for wearable devices, the wearing direction or position should be constant. Some existing studies have controlled the experimental environment when collecting dog behavior data, so the collection method's performance may degrade in real-life applications [1]. To reduce the noise of the data collected in such an environment, preprocessing and analysis methods suitable for the characteristics of the data are also required; however, this is only a supplementary method.

To address this problem, multiple, rather than single types of data can be used. The fusion of multiple data types makes it possible to complement data noise and improve the accuracy of the behavior recognition of dogs. In research on human behavior recognition, various behavior recognition studies using multiple data have already been conducted [6]; however, there have been few behavior recognition studies for dogs.

Accordingly, this paper proposes behavior recognition that combines multimodal data to estimate the amount of activity for the most commonly raised dogs. For this purpose, we aimed to recognize seven behaviors (standing, sitting, lying with raised head, lying without raised head, walking, sniffing, and running) with video data from a camera and sensor data (acceleration, gyroscope) from a wearable device.

The main contributions of this paper are:

1. Exploration of a suitable dog detection method using video data by comparing object detection methods (FasterRCNN, YOLOv3, YOLOv4) mainly used in computer vision.
2. Exploration of the combination of statistical characteristics that affect the recognition of dog behavior using sensor data (acceleration, gyroscope) collected from wearable devices.
3. Comparison of the performance of the existing method using single data and the method that fuses multimodal data and exploration of the model for dog behavior recognition improvement through performance comparison between deep learning-based fusion models (CNN, LSTM, CNN-LSTM).

2. Related Works

2.1. Behavior Recognition Based on Multimodal Data

Research on behavior recognition has been progressing rapidly and has focused mostly on humans. Most existing studies on behavior recognition have focused on images [7,8]. However, due to problems with various shooting environments and hardware resource problems, most studies use sensors that are cheaper and have a high computational efficiency [9–11].

In recent years, multimodal data-based studies have been gradually increasing in number to improve the accuracy of behavior recognition. Among them, the study of behavior recognition through the fusion of various sensor data were focused on and the accuracy was improved when using multiple-sensor data compared to single-sensor data [6]. In general, accelerometer and gyroscope data are often used in behavior recognition. Steels et al. performed badminton behavior recognition using accelerometer and gyroscope data, and the accuracy of most actions such as drive, smash, and net drop was improved [12]. Uddin et al. proposed a behavior recognition system for health management that required wearing electrocardiogram (ECG) sensors, accelerometers, and gyroscope sensors on the chest, wrist, and ankle [13].

Furthermore, studies based on multimodal data that combine different types of data have been conducted. Fusing these different types of data can complement the quality of data, which can have a good effect on performance. Ehatisham Ul Haq et al. proposed a multimodal feature feature-level fusion approach for human behavior recognition using RGB cameras, depth sensors, and wearable inertial sensors, and the accuracy was improved when data of RGB cameras, accelerometers, and gyroscopes was fused [9].

Behavior recognition based on multimodal data that fuses these different types of data requires deep learning techniques that can automatically extract abstract features for each data type. Accordingly, multilayer perceptron (MLP), convolutional neural networks (CNNs), and recurrent neural networks (RNNs) are widely used to study behavior recognition and show higher performance than existing methods [7,14–16].

Accordingly, this paper collected multimodal data using a camera and a wearable device and fused them based on the abovementioned studies to obtain behavior recognition. In addition, we used a deep learning-based model to extract features from multimodal data.

2.2. Dog Behavior Recognition

Pet behavior recognition research is important for understanding the condition of pets. Various studies are being conducted to check the status of pets in daily life such as their activity and sleep or to predict diseases using medical data [17]. Among them, the study of dog behavior recognition can be divided into cases using video data and cases using sensor data.

Research using video data can be further divided into research to detect dogs and research to extract joint motion. For dog detection, data collection and analysis are only easy when the shooting location is fixed, so a camera is generally attached to the ceiling to observe the dog's movements. Bleuer Elsner et al. analyzed movement patterns in dogs with attention-deficit/hyperactivity disorder (ADHD)-like behavior, which they observed by installing a camera on the ceiling [3]. However, when the camera was attached to the ceiling, only the movement and speed of the dog could be identified [3]. Furthermore, research is also being conducted to recognize the behavior of livestock animals such as pigs, cows, and horses [18].

Research on the skeletons of dogs is focused on pose estimation. The 3D position of dogs can be estimated using Kinect, a camera that can recognize depth and is mainly composed of RGB and IR cameras. Kearney et al. proposed a markerless approach for 3D canine pose estimation from RGBD images using the Kinect v2 [19]. Pereira et al. proposed SLEAP, a multi-animal pose tracking framework for living things ranging from insects to vertebrates [20].

In studies using these video data, overlap with other objects significantly lowers the recognition accuracy. In addition, since behavior recognition is only possible within the shooting radius, it is difficult to target dogs at home unless the entire house is photographed with cameras.

In comparison, studies using sensor data generally collect data by strapping a wearable device onto a dog. Currently, commercialized devices such as Fitbark, Petpace, and Whistle have been released and are used for tracking dogs' activity; these are mainly used to increase the activity of dogs and improve their health [21].

The appropriate location for the device to be worn—such as the neck, stomach, legs, or tail—has been extensively studied; it is important to select an appropriate location because a poor choice can cause discomfort to the dog. Most commercially available devices are worn around the neck [22,23], which has relatively less noise than other locations [24]. In addition, when examining the behavior types of dogs, most commercialized dog wearable devices have an accelerometer sensor to estimate the dog's behavior [22]. Since a single sensor is used, the activity level of dogs is divided into three to five levels rather than more sophisticated behavior recognition. Recently, more detailed behavior recognition has become possible because gyroscope sensor data can be integrated and analyzed, but it is difficult to obtain high recognition accuracy for all behaviors.

Table 1 summarizes previous studies of dog behavior recognition using video data or sensor data. To date, there have been many machine learning-based behavior recognition studies, but research has been conducted by collecting either only video or sensor data. There are studies on behavior recognition based on multimodal data that embed various sensors in wearable devices, but fusing it with other types of data can improve the accuracy, and if data noise occurs, it can be compensated. Accordingly, in this paper, we aimed to improve the behavior recognition accuracy of dogs by solving the problems of existing studies through deep learning-based fusion of sensor data and video data.

Table 1. Summary of dog behavior recognition studies using a camera or wearable device.

Paper	Using Video Data	Using Sensor Data Position	Acc	Gyro	Number of Behaviors	Machine Learning	Deep Learning
[1]		Neck	O		10		O
[2]		Neck	O		3	O	
[23]		Neck Tail	O	O	7	O	
[25]		Neck Back	O	O	7	O	
[26]	O				10		O
This paper	O	Neck	O	O	7		O

3. Dog Behavior Recognition Based on Multimodal Data

In this study, we propose dog behavior recognition based on multimodal data. The purpose of this study was to find a method to improve the behavior recognition accuracy of dogs. This was performed to estimate the specific amount of activity of dogs. We limited our analysis to the most common dog breed, and we used a commonly used camera and wearable device. We assumed that the camera was installed in a place where the dog can be seen easily with minimal overlapping of other objects inside or outside the house and the wearable device was a collar.

Table 2 illustrates seven behaviors to recognize: standing, sitting, lying with raised head, lying without raised head, walking, sniffing, and running. Although dogs display various behaviors in daily life, such as eating and shaking, the behaviors representing the amount of activity of dogs were selected after referring to existing studies on dog behavior recognition [1,2,25,26]. In addition, since the wearable device is worn on the neck, it is sensitive to the movement of the head. In this paper, the criterion for lying was divided by whether the head was raised. Since the shortest length of each behavior is 4 s, it was processed by generating behavior sequence data for 4 s segments.

Figure 1 describes the overall process of data collection, data preprocessing, and dog behavior recognition. First, behavior data on videos and sensors were collected through cameras and wearable devices, followed by data preprocessing. For the video data, a dog was detected in a frame, missing values that were not detected were processed; for sensor data, outliers were removed, and missing values were processed. After that, the two types of data were synchronized based on time to generate behavior sequence data. These data were input into the proposed fusion model, which then learned to recognize dog behavior. The following subsections describe the details of each step.

Table 2. Dog behavior to be recognized.

Behavior Code	Behavior	Description
B1	Standing	Standing still with all four legs touching the ground.
B2	Sitting	The buttocks touch the floor without the stomach touching the floor.
B3	Lying with raised head	Lying down on the floor with their side, back, or stomach on the floor with their head raised.
B4	Lying without raised head	Lying down the floor with their side, back, or stomach on the floor without raising their head.
B5	Walking	Moving forward with four legs moving (three legs touching the ground).
B6	Sniffing	Moving or stopping with light head movement and the nose close to the ground.
B7	Running	Moving forward with legs moving simultaneously at a faster speed than walking.

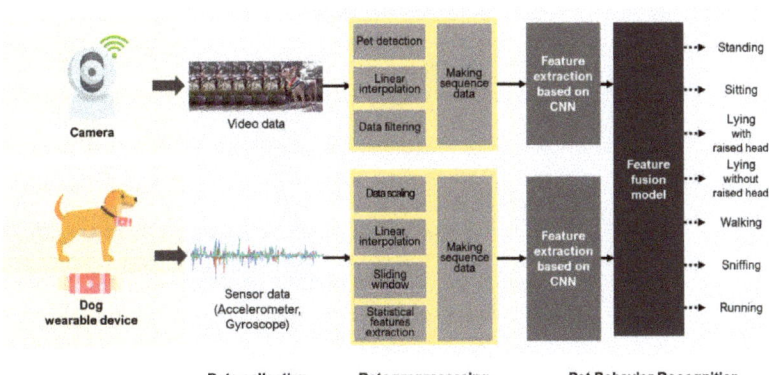

Figure 1. Process of dog behavior recognition based on multimodal data.

3.1. Video Data Collection and Preprocessing

The video data were used to check the movement area of the dog, and an IP camera was used to capture the front or side view of the dog. Data were collected at 20 FPS with a resolution of 1920 × 1080.

Since various objects such as the owner or dog products appeared in the collected video data, dog detection was performed to check only the movement of dogs. Currently, various methods have been proposed for object detection in computer vision; however, detecting a distant dog inside a house requires a method with good performance at small object detection. Among the representative small object detection methods, Liu compared the performance of methods such as YOLOv3, FasterRCNN, and SSD [27]. In addition, Nguyen compared the performance of RetinaNet, Fast RCNN, YOLOv3, and FasterRCNN [28]. In terms of processing speed, it was confirmed that the performances of Faster RCNN and YOLOv3 were excellent. Accordingly, in this paper, we performed dog detection by adding FasterRCNN, YOLOv3, and YOLOv4, which has improved performance over YOLOv3 [29].

The collected data were sliced into 4-s units, and the result of dog detection for each frame was the center coordinates (x, y), width, and height of the detected bounding box. However, it is difficult to detect dogs in various shooting environments every time. For the learning model, if all data for undetected frames is removed, the learning performance may be degraded, so it is necessary to process missing values. For this purpose, missing values were replaced using linear interpolation, which is one of the most widely used methods because of its simplicity and low computational cost. Since the length of the video data were not long, even if the missing values were continuous, if there were detected bounding boxes before and after the missing values, it was set to be interpolated to replace the missing values. If 50% or more of the values for one video were missing, the data were filtered because the reliability of the data would be lost even if the missing values were replaced.

3.2. Sensor Data Collection and Preprocessing

The collected sensor data were three-axis accelerometer and three-axis gyroscope da-ta taken once per second from a wearable device placed on the neck of a dog. The collected data were scaled using the median and quartiles values to minimize the influence of outliers on data collected from the wearable device. Next, an upsampling process was performed for each time-series index to display the collected data as a sequence. In the communication process, it was also necessary to process missing values for the time not collected because of the possibility that some data may have been lost. As with the video data, the missing values were replaced using linear interpolation. The sensor data had a shorter length, so to interpolate only data for 1 s out of 4 s, the number of consecutively interpolating missing values was limited to one. Next, for input into the learning model, the sensor data were divided into 4-s windows through a sliding window.

Next, we proceeded with feature extraction. Feature extraction can generally be divided into handcrafting features and learning features. Handcrafting features require little computation and can be easily extracted, but the sensor type is specific and feature selection is required, whereas learning features automatically learn features from raw data and are robust, but it is difficult to adjust parameters and interpret learned features [8]. Accordingly, we want to improve the behavior recognition accuracy by extracting handcrafting features and reflecting them in the learning model.

In several studies, statistical features have been extracted and used for behavior recognition; however, this study only used features with little computation because complex features were automatically extracted and input into the next step, a fusion model. The features (f) selected in this study were the mean (f_{mean}), variance (f_{var}), standard deviation (f_{std}), amplitude (f_{amp}), and skewness (f_{skew}); their equations are (1)–(5) for data length n and data value x. These features were counted 30 times for the three axes of the accelerometer and three axes of the gyroscope, and these features became the input values of the fusion model together with the raw data to determine how much they affect dog behavior recognition accuracy.

$$f_{mean} = \frac{1}{n}\sum_{i=1}^{n} x_i \tag{1}$$

$$f_{var} = \frac{1}{n}\sum (x - \bar{x})^2 \tag{2}$$

$$f_{std} = \sqrt{\frac{1}{n}\sum (x - \bar{x})^2} \tag{3}$$

$$f_{amp} = \max(x) - \min(x) \tag{4}$$

$$f_{skew} = \frac{\frac{1}{n}\sum_{i=1}^{n}(x_i - \bar{x})^3}{\left(\frac{1}{n}\sum_{i=1}^{n}(x_i - \bar{x})^2\right)^{\frac{3}{2}}} \tag{5}$$

3.3. Dog Behavior Recognition

Figure 2 describes the model based on the multimodal data for dog behavior recognition extracted the features of video data and sensor data and then merged the extracted data to recognize behaviors.

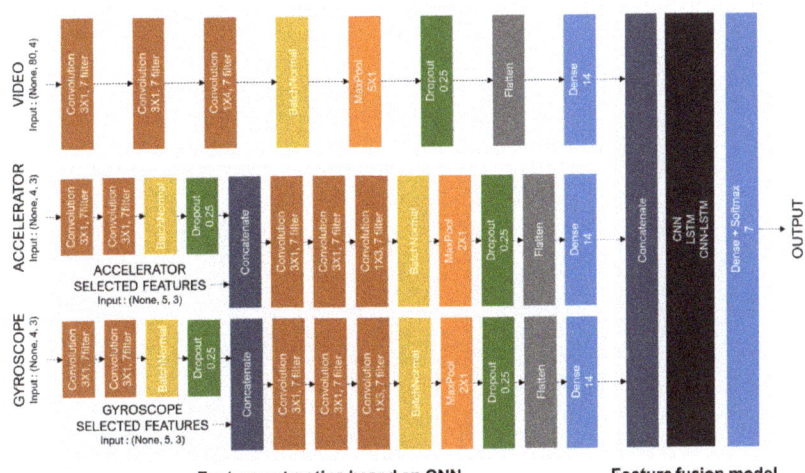

Figure 2. Overall model structure based on the multimodal data for dog behavior recognition.

3.3.1. Feature Extraction

Feature extraction uses CNN, which performs a convolution operation. CNNs can extract high-level features from both time-series data and video data. In this study, we extracted features using CNN for both video data and sensor data, which required us to conduct feature extraction separately.

Since the feature extraction of video data were 80 4-s frames, we focused on reducing the frame dimension. The convolution operation consists of seven filters of size (3, 1) and proceeds three times through the ReLU activation function, after which batch normalization is performed. Then, after max-pooling with (5, 1) size, dropout is performed at a rate of 0.25 to prevent overfitting. Finally, the extracted features are flattened to perform dense layer and batch normalization.

Feature extraction for sensor data were performed by dividing the accelerator and gyroscope. First, the raw data and the selected features are concatenated. Next, the convolution operation is performed twice with size (3, 1) and once with size (1, 3). The first two are for dimensionality reduction for features, and the last is dimensionality reduction for three axes. Then, after batch normalization, maxpooling of size (2, 1) is performed, and dropout is performed at a rate of 0.25. Finally, through flattening of the extracted features, the dense layer and batch normalization are performed. For the gyroscope data, the same process was performed. Finally, the extracted features of the accelerator and gyroscope are concatenated again.

3.3.2. Feature Fusion Model for Dog Behavior Recognition

Next, the extracted features were fused and classified to recognize dog behaviors. We used CNN, LSTM, and CNN-LSTM models, which are the most commonly used deep learning methods. LSTM is a type of RNN that is specialized for time-series and improves the vanishing gradient problem of RNN. Furthermore, a recent hybrid method of CNN and LSTM has shown good performance in feature extraction considering time-series and is being used in research on prediction and classification in various fields. The structures of the CNN, LSTM, and CNN-LSTM models constructed in this study are shown in Figure 3. As the final step of all models, softmax was performed for multiple behavior recognition to derive behavior-specific probabilities.

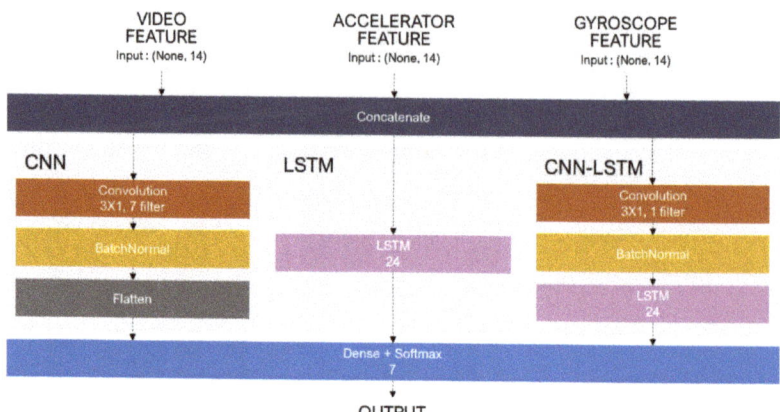

Figure 3. Model structures of CNN, LSTM, and CNN-LSTM for feature fusion.

4. Experiments

4.1. Experimental Setup

This study was implemented using Keras as a backend with TensorFlow as a Python language. Table 3 shows the detailed experimental specifications of this study.

Table 3. Experimental specifications.

Metric	Description
CPU	Intel Core i7-8700K
GPU	NVIDIA GeForce RTX 3080
RAM	32 GB
Python	3.8
TensorFlow	2.4.1
Keras	2.5.0

4.1.1. Data Collection Process and Dataset

The experiment was conducted with one dog: a 4-year-old male Yorkshire terrier. Data collection was conducted in compliance with animal ethics. To obtain consent from the owner and to eliminate the dog's anxiety, the collection was always carried out in situations where the owner accompanied the dog. In addition, to reflect the environment in daily life as much as possible, natural behaviors, not trained behaviors, were observed within the radius captured by the camera. Among the data collected in this process, behaviors that were externally influenced, other than self-moving behaviors such as petting or touching the dog, were removed through filtering. In addition, the total time for collection of data did not exceed 20 min to ensure that the health of the dog was not affected.

To make the collection environment as similar as possible to the environment in daily life, there were no restrictions on the space inside the house, such as the living room or outdoor space, and a camera was installed so that the front or side of the dog could be seen. In addition, to increase the detection rate of the dog in the video, videos were not taken from too far away. The IP camera used was the HejHome Smart Home Camera pro, and the resolution was Full HD (1920 × 1080) and 20 FPS. Figure 4 describes the process of collecting sensor data from a manufactured wearable device based on the Arduino nano 33 IoT board. The wearable device was manufactured as a collar. Data were collected from the server through Bluetooth with an Android-based smart device. The accelerometer and gyroscope data were collected using the LSM6DS3 module.

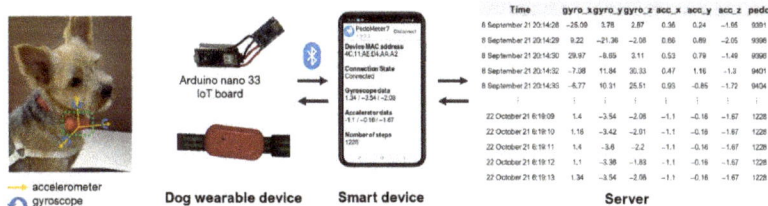

Figure 4. The process of collecting sensor data from a manufactured wearable device.

The collected data were matched based on the time of the video data and the sensor data, and cases where even one of the two data were not collected were excluded. In the collected dataset, the behavior of the dog was determined based on the video, and the behavior was labeled. The collected and pre-processed dataset is shown in Table 4. To reduce the data imbalance, the most frequently collected behavior, sitting, was set as 30 differences from the second-largest behavior. For learning, 80% of the entire dataset was used as the training dataset, the rest was used for the test dataset, and 20% of the training dataset was used for the validation dataset.

Table 4. Experimental dataset.

Behavior	FasterRCNN		YOLOv3		YOLOv4	
	Training	Test	Training	Test	Training	Test
Standing	89	22	96	24	98	24
Sitting	132	34	144	37	142	36
Lying with raised head	99	25	121	30	105	26
Lying without raised head	109	27	111	28	103	26
Sniffing	29	7	44	11	48	12
Walking	57	14	101	25	118	30
Running	8	2	31	8	54	13
Total	523	131	648	163	668	167

4.1.2. Performance Evaluation Measurement and Method

Performance evaluation was compared by measuring the accuracy, precision, recall, and f-score. Accuracy represents the ratio of correctly recognized numbers among all N pieces of data. Precision is the ratio of the prediction and the actual value of the positive data among the positive prediction data and is defined in Equation (6). Recall is the ratio of prediction and actual positive data among actual positive data and is defined as Equation (7). The final f-score was calculated as the harmonic average of precision and recall, as shown in Equation (8). In addition, various model evaluations were conducted with 100 epochs and a batch size of 16. Adam was used as the optimizer, and the learning rate was set to 0.001.

$$Precision = \frac{True\ Positive}{True\ Positive + False\ Positive} \quad (6)$$

$$Recall = \frac{True\ Positive}{True\ Positive + False\ Negative} \quad (7)$$

$$F-score = 2 \times \frac{Precision \times Recall}{Precision + Recall} \quad (8)$$

4.2. Experimental Results

The experiment had three goals. The first was to find a suitable dog detection method by comparing the performance of object detection methods using video data. The second was to find the combination of statistical features that affect the behavioral recognition of dogs by comparing the performance using sensor data. The third was to compare the performance difference methods that use single data and those that fuse multimodal data and to determine the proper model for improving dog behavior recognition through performance comparison of deep learning-based fusion models.

4.2.1. Behavior Recognition Using Video Data

For the video data, FasterRCNN, YOLOv3, and YOLOv4 were used to check the dog detection rate. To confirm the detection rate, an experiment was conducted using a pre-trained model with the COCO dataset in three dog detection methods. Figure 5 displays one of the detected results for "sitting". YOLOv4 detected the dog's size better than the other methods. Figure 6 shows the detection distribution according to the amount of data. YOLOv3 had the largest amount of data with a 100% detection rate and the largest amount of data with a 0% detection rate. On average, FasterRCNN's detection rate was 68.62%, YOLOv3's was 67.13%, and YOLOv4 had the highest detection rate at 72.01%. Figure 7 shows the detection distribution by behavior. Overall, the recognition rate was high when the dog performed B2 behavior, and the detection rate was the lowest when the dog performed B7 behavior.

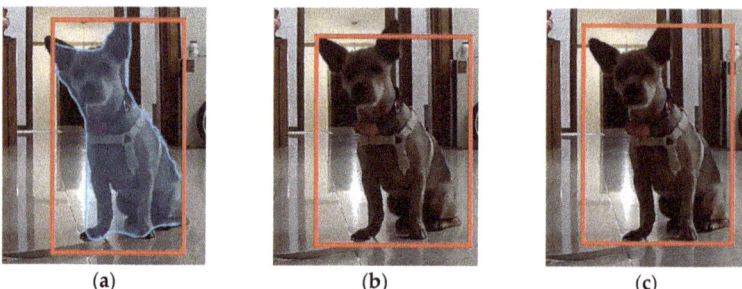

Figure 5. Result of dog detection for "sitting": (a) FasterRCNN; (b) YOLOv3; (c) YOLOv4.

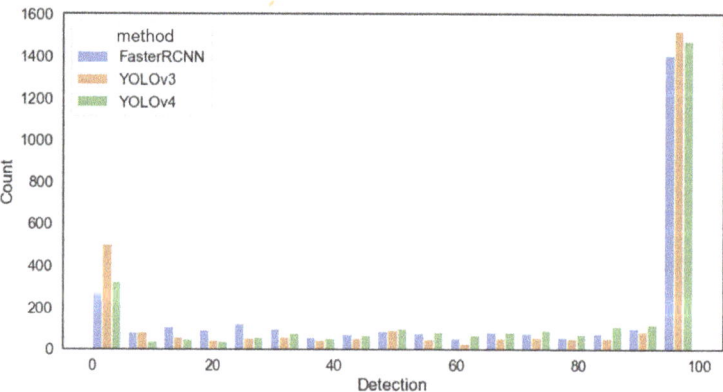

Figure 6. Distribution of detection by method according to the amount of data.

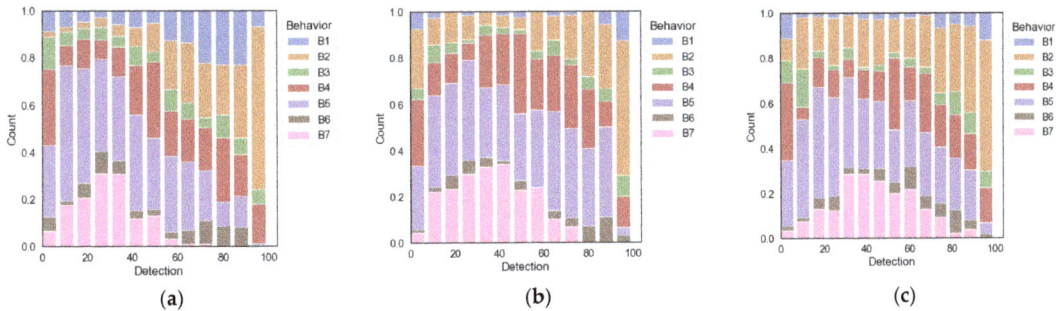

Figure 7. Distribution of detection by dog behavior per method: (**a**) FasterRCNN; (**b**) YOLOv3; (**c**) YOLOv4.

Table 5 shows the performance evaluation results for behavior recognition with the object detection method using only video data. On average, the accuracy was 86.7%, and among the methods, YOLOv4 had the highest accuracy (89.2%). Figure 8 shows the fusion matrix of behavior recognition by behavior. In general, B1–B4, which did not involve movement, had a high recognition rate. In contrast, in the case of B7, since the B7 data of FasterRCNN were too small compared to that of YOLOv3 and YOLOv4, it was judged that YOLOv3 and YOLOv4 were relatively well aware of running, whereas FasterRCNN was not.

Table 5. Results of behavior recognition performance evaluation by dog detection methods using video data.

Dog Detection Method	Accuracy	Precision	Recall	F-Score
FasterRCNN	86.3%	0.91	0.86	0.88
YOLOv3	84.7%	0.9	0.85	0.86
YOLOv4	**89.2%**	**0.92**	**0.89**	**0.9**
Average	86.7%	0.91	0.87	0.88

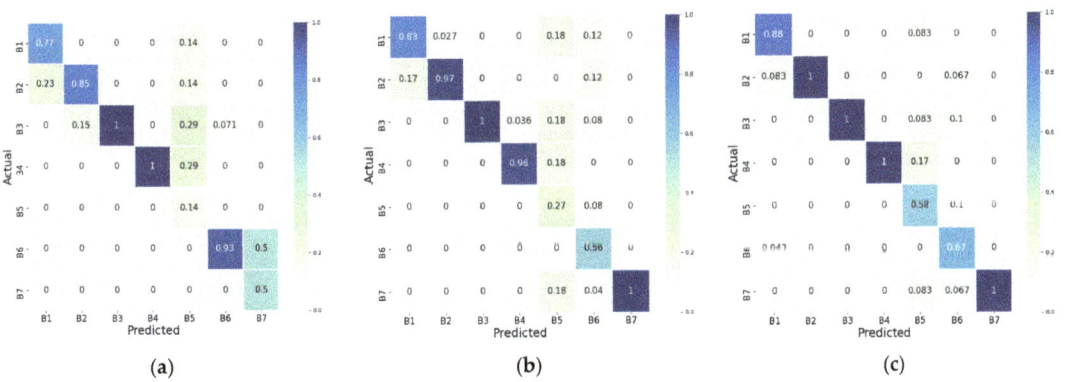

Figure 8. Confusion matrix of behavior recognition by dog detection methods using video data: (**a**) FasterRCNN; (**b**) YOLOv3; (**c**) YOLOv4. The bluer the cell, the higher the accuracy of dog recognition.

4.2.2. Behavior Recognition Using Sensor Data

Experiments on sensor data were conducted by combining the five statistical features specified in Section 3.2, and it was confirmed which combination of features had the greatest effect on performance. Table 6 shows the experimental results for the case where no features were selected (None), those for the single-feature case, and the ten feature combinations that showed the best performance among multiple features from a total of 32 feature combinations.

Table 6. Results of behavior recognition performance evaluation by selected features using sensor data.

Selected Features	Feature Length	Accuracy	Precision	Recall	F-Score
None	6	0.455	0.56	0.46	0.49
f_{mean}	12	0.383	0.6	0.38	0.46
f_{var}	12	0.443	0.76	0.44	0.48
f_{std}	12	0.509	0.62	0.51	0.55
f_{amp}	12	0.479	0.63	0.48	0.54
f_{skew}	12	0.395	0.66	0.4	0.47
$f_{mean} + f_{amp}$	18	0.521	0.63	0.52	0.56
$f_{var} + f_{amp}$	18	0.515	0.62	0.51	0.54
$f_{amp} + f_{skew}$	18	0.515	0.63	0.51	0.55
$f_{mean} + f_{amp} + f_{skew}$	24	0.515	0.61	0.51	0.55
$f_{std} + f_{amp} + f_{skew}$	24	0.551	0.63	0.55	0.57
$f_{mean} + f_{var} + f_{std} + f_{amp}$	30	0.503	0.68	0.5	0.56
$f_{mean} + f_{var} + f_{std} + f_{skew}$	30	0.551	0.7	0.55	0.61
$f_{mean} + f_{std} + f_{amp} + f_{skew}$	30	0.539	0.61	0.54	0.56
$f_{var} + f_{std} + f_{amp} + f_{skew}$	30	0.539	0.67	0.54	0.58
$f_{mean} + f_{var} + f_{std} + f_{amp} + f_{skew}$	36	**0.563**	**0.76**	**0.56**	**0.62**

As a single feature, f_{std} performed well, but when combined with other features, f_{amp} was the best complementary feature. In contrast, f_{var} degraded performance or did not affect performance. In the case of multiple features, since the degree of complementation between features was different, there was a difference in performance even when features were similarly combined; however, the performance was generally improved when $f_{amp} + f_{skew}$ was included. As a result, the combination of multiple features elicited better performance than the result using only raw data. Among them, the combination that showed the best performance was $f_{mean} + f_{var} + f_{std} + f_{amp} + f_{skew}$, which showed an accuracy of 56.3%.

Figure 9 shows the confusion matrix for None with no features selected and for the best feature combination in Table 6. The sensor data showed that behavior recognition for B4 and B6 was well achieved, and it was confirmed that the recognition rate for B2 was improved when statistical features were included. Since the device worn around the neck was sensitive to the movement of the head, it is judged that the recognition rate was high because these behaviors feature fewer head movements than other behaviors.

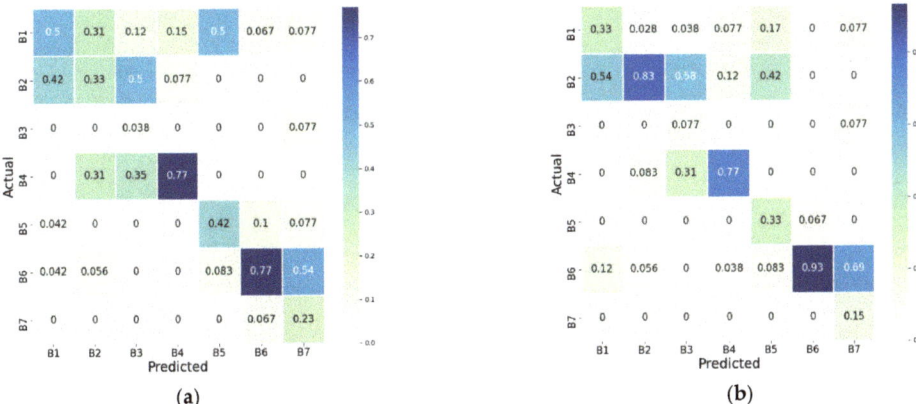

(a) (b)

Figure 9. Confusion matrix of behavior recognition by selected features using sensor data: (a) Confusion matrix with no selected features; (b) Confusion matrix with selected features of $f_{mean} + f_{var} + f_{std} + f_{amp} + f_{skew}$.

4.2.3. Dog Behavior Recognition Based on Multimodal Data

The performance evaluation of the fusion model was performed on the fusion models CNN, LSTM, and CNN-LSTM for each dog detection method. In addition, a model that only concatenated the extracted features for each set of data were added to the performance evaluation to compare the results of single data and multimodal data models.

Experimental results are shown in Table 7. Compared with the performance when using only a single data type in Sections 4.2.1 and 4.2.2, it was confirmed that the average performance was improved by about 90.3% when the data were integrated. Among the fusion models for each dog detection method, the CNN-LSTM model showed higher accuracy than other fusion models. In particular, in the case of YOLOv4, which had the highest behavior recognition accuracy using video data, the CNN-LSTM model showed the highest accuracy at about 93.4%. The performance of the CNN model and the LSTM model is expected to improve slightly if they had as deep layers as the CNN-LSTM model.

Table 7. Results of behavior recognition performance evaluation by fusion models based on multimodal data.

Dog Detection Method	Fusion Model	Measure			
		Accuracy	Precision	Recall	F-Score
FasterRCNN	Only concatenate	0.885	0.89	0.89	0.89
	CNN	0.855	0.88	0.85	0.86
	LSTM	0.885	0.91	0.89	0.89
	CNN-LSTM	0.924	0.94	0.92	0.93
YOLOv3	Only concatenate	0.908	0.92	0.91	0.91
	CNN	0.926	0.94	0.93	0.93
	LSTM	0.914	0.92	0.91	0.92
	CNN-LSTM	0.920	0.93	0.92	0.92
YOLOv4	Only concatenate	0.904	0.91	0.9	0.9
	CNN	0.898	0.91	0.9	0.9
	LSTM	0.880	0.9	0.88	0.88
	CNN-LSTM	**0.934**	0.94	0.93	0.93
Average		0.903	0.92	0.90	0.91

Figure 10 shows the confusion matrix for each fusion model. The recognition rate for all behaviors is improved overall compared to the case of using single data. However, among them, the behavior recognition rate for B5 and B7 is slightly low. FasterRCNN, which showed a very lower recognition rate for B5 and B7 when using only video data, improved when using multimodal data, but still shows low numbers as shown in Figure 10a. Even with the CNN-LSTM model, FasterRCNN had a low behavior recognition rate for B5 and B7 as shown in Figure 10d, whereas YOLOv3 and YOLOv4 significantly improved the behavior recognition rate with the CNN-LSTM model as shown in Figure 10e,f.

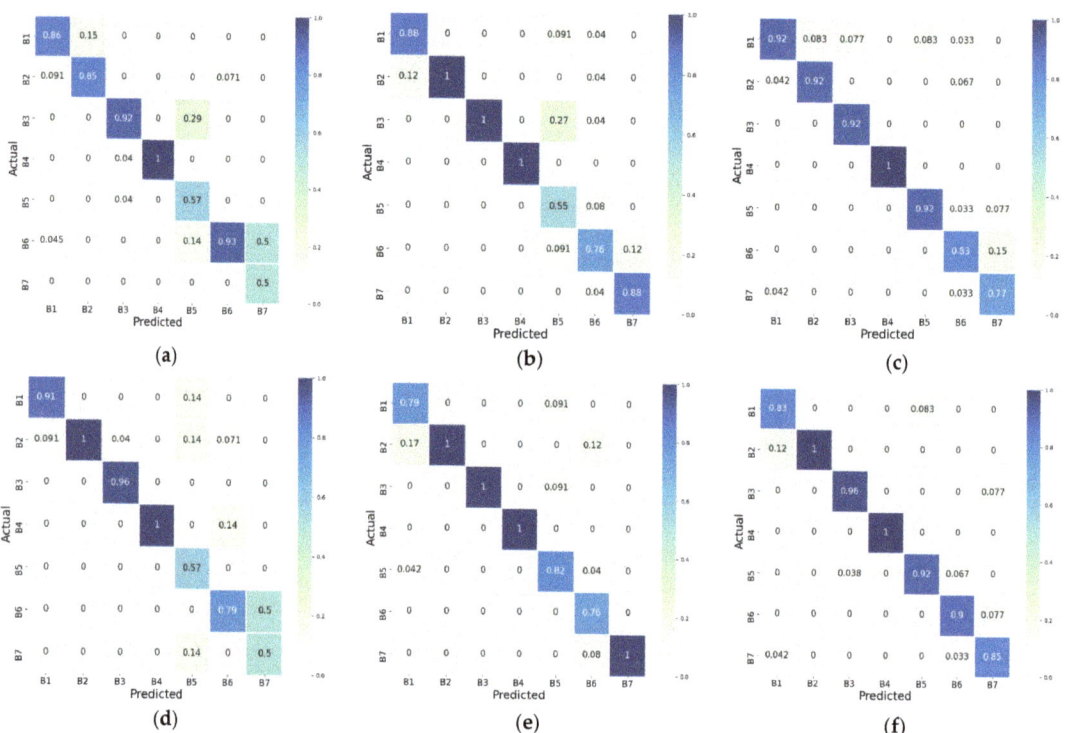

Figure 10. Confusion matrix of behavior recognition by fusion models based on multimodal data: (**a**) Only concatenate model with FasterRCNN; (**b**) Only concatenate model with YOLOv3; (**c**) Only concatenate model with YOLOv4; (**d**) CNN-LSTM model with FasterRCNN; (**e**) CNN-LSTM model with YOLOv3; (**f**) CNN-LSTM model with YOLOv4.

Since some aspects of sniffing may look similar to standing or walking, and walking has similar appearances to running except for speed, it is thought that detailed feature extraction is necessary to improve the accuracy of behavior recognition. Since the model structure proposed in this paper is not an optimal model for behavior recognition of dogs, if the model is improved, such as by increasing the layer depth or finding an appropriate hyperparameter, the recognition rate of all behaviors will probably be improved.

5. Conclusions

This paper proposed a multimodal data-based behavior recognition of dogs by fusing video data from a camera and sensor data (accelerator, gyroscope) from a wearable device. The collected data were about dogs, and seven types of behavior (standing, sitting, lying with raised head, lying without raised head, walking, sniffing, and running) were recognized after preprocessing according to the characteristics of each data type.

In the case of video data, FasterRCNN, YOLOv3, and YOLOv4, which are representative object detection methods, were used to identify the movement area of dogs. Among them, YOLOv4 had the highest dog detection rate and the best behavior recognition performance. Because behavior recognition was performed by extracting the detected area, the object detection rate and the accuracy of behavior recognition had a high correlation. In the case of sensor data, accelerator and gyroscope data were collected using a wearable device manufactured based on Arduino, and various statistical feature extraction methods were used. When two or more features were used rather than a single feature, high performance was generally achieved, and the combination of the features with the highest performance among them—the mean, variance, standard deviation, amplitude, and skewness—were all combined. Finally, multimodal data-based CNN, LSTM, and CNN-LSTM models were used to evaluate and compare performance with existing single data-based models. When the video data and the sensor data were fused, the average accuracy was about 90.3%, and the multimodal data-based models showed improved performance over that of the single data-based models. In particular, when the CNN-LSTM model was used, the performance was good, and the case of dog detection using YOLOv4 was the highest at about 93.4%.

In the process of carrying out this study, it was confirmed that there was a difference in the recognition rate for each behavior in the results of the case where only video data were used compared to the case where only sensor data were used. In the case of video data, the recognition rate was high when there was no movement, such as standing, sitting, lying with raised head, and lying without raised head. The recognition rate for running was also high. Unlike sniffing and walking, running generally does not feature di-rection change within 4 s, so it is probably judged that the feature was differentiated from other behaviors. In the case of sensor data, the recognition rate for sitting, lying without raised head, and walking was high, and the behaviors with little change in the head movement were well recognized. Finally, the recognition rate for all behaviors overall increased as the two data complemented each other for the multimodal data-based models.

Since optimizing the model was not the purpose of the study, we proceeded with one dog, but in the future, data collection according to breed and size is required to reflect the properties of various dogs. This study can be applied for the treatment or health monitoring of dogs, and among them, it is expected to provide a simple way to estimate the amount of activity. Various diseases such as obesity and depression can be identified through changes in the activity level of dogs. To this end, if the data collection cycle is changed or the model layer (number of layers, appropriate hyperparameters, etc.) is changed, then the performance can be improved compared to the results found in this study. In the future, to improve the accuracy of dog behavior recognition, we plan to find an optimal fusion model and expand the behavior types.

Author Contributions: Conceptualization, J.K. and N.M.; methodology, J.K. and N.M.; software, J.K.; validation, J.K.; formal analysis, J.K. and N.M.; investigation, J.K. and N.M.; resources, J.K.; data curation, J.K. and N.M.; writing—original draft preparation, J.K.; writing—review and editing, J.K. and N.M.; visualization, J.K.; supervision, N.M.; project administration, N.M.; funding acquisition, N.M. All authors have read and agreed to the published version of the manuscript.

Funding: This research was supported by the National Research Foundation of Korea (NRF) grant funded by the Korea government (MSIT) (No. 2021R1A2C2011966).

Institutional Review Board Statement: The animal study protocol was approved by the Institutional Animal Care and Use Committee of Hoseo University IACUC (protocol code: HSUIACUC-22-006(2)).

Informed Consent Statement: Not applicable.

Data Availability Statement: The data presented in this study are available from the corresponding author upon request. The data are not publicly available due to privacy and ethical concerns.

Conflicts of Interest: The authors declare no conflict of interest.

References

1. Chambers, R.D.; Yoder, N.C.; Carson, A.B.; Junge, C.; Allen, D.E.; Prescott, L.M.; Bradley, S.; Wymore, G.; Lloyd, K.; Lyle, S. Deep Learning Classification of Canine Behavior Using a Single Collar-Mounted Accelerometer: Real-World Validation. *Animals* **2021**, *11*, 1549. [CrossRef] [PubMed]
2. Griffies, J.D.; Zutty, J.; Sarzen, M.; Soorholtz, S. Wearable Sensor Shown to Specifically Quantify Pruritic Behaviors in Dogs. *BMC Vet. Res.* **2018**, *14*, 124. [CrossRef] [PubMed]
3. Bleuer-Elsner, S.; Zamansky, A.; Fux, A.; Kaplun, D.; Romanov, S.; Sinitca, A.; Masson, S.; van der Linden, D. Computational Analysis of Movement Patterns of Dogs with ADHD-Like Behavior. *Animals* **2019**, *9*, 1140. [CrossRef]
4. Stephan, G.; Leidhold, J.; Hammerschmidt, K. Pet Dogs Home Alone: A Video-Based Study. *Appl. Anim. Behav. Sci.* **2021**, *244*, 105463. [CrossRef]
5. Colpoys, J.; DeCock, D. Evaluation of the FitBark Activity Monitor for Measuring Physical Activity in Dogs. *Animals* **2021**, *11*, 781. [CrossRef] [PubMed]
6. Nweke, H.F.; Teh, Y.W.; Mujtaba, G.; Alo, U.R.; Al-garadi, M.A. Multi-Sensor Fusion Based on Multiple Classifier Systems for Human Activity Identification. *Hum. Cent. Comput. Inf. Sci.* **2019**, *9*, 34. [CrossRef]
7. Dang, L.M.; Min, K.; Wang, H.; Piran, M.J.; Lee, C.H.; Moon, H. Sensor-Based and Vision-Based Human Activity Recognition: A Comprehensive. *Survey Pattern Recognit.* **2020**, *108*, 107561. [CrossRef]
8. Wang, Y.; Cang, S.; Yu, H. A Survey on Wearable Sensor Modality Centred Human Activity Recognition in Health Care. *Expert Syst. Appl.* **2019**, *137*, 167–190. [CrossRef]
9. Ehatisham-Ul-Haq, M.; Javed, A.; Azam, M.A.; Malik, H.M.A.; Irtaza, A.; Lee, I.H.; Mahmood, M.T. Robust Human Activity Recognition Using Multimodal Feature-Level Fusion. *IEEE Access* **2019**, *7*, 60736–60751. [CrossRef]
10. Khowaja, S.A.; Yahya, B.N.; Lee, S.L. CAPHAR: Context-Aware Personalized Human Activity Recognition Using Associative Learning in Smart Environments. *Hum. Cent. Comput. Inf. Sci.* **2020**, *10*, 35. [CrossRef]
11. Gerina, F.; Massa, S.M.; Moi, F.; Reforgiato Recupero, D.; Riboni, D. Recognition of Cooking Activities through Air Quality Sensor Data for Supporting Food Journaling. *Hum. Cent. Comput. Inf. Sci.* **2020**, *10*, 27. [CrossRef]
12. Steels, T.; Van Herbruggen, B.; Fontaine, J.; De Pessemier, T.; Plets, D.; De Poorter, E. Badminton Activity Recognition Using Accelerometer Data. *Sensors* **2020**, *20*, 4685. [CrossRef] [PubMed]
13. Uddin, M.Z.; Hassan, M.M.; Alsanad, A.; Savaglio, C. A Body Sensor Data Fusion and Deep Recurrent Neural Network-Based Behavior Recognition Approach for Robust Healthcare. *Inf. Fusion* **2020**, *55*, 105–115. [CrossRef]
14. Cicceri, G.; De Vita, F.; Bruneo, D.; Merlino, G.; Puliafito, A. A Deep Learning Approach for Pressure Ulcer Prevention Using Wearable Computing. *Hum. Cent. Comput. Inf. Sci.* **2020**, *10*, 5. [CrossRef]
15. Malik, S.; Ullah, I.; Kim, D.; Lee, K. Heuristic and Statistical Prediction Algorithms Survey for Smart Environments. *J. Inf. Process. Syst.* **2020**, *16*, 1196–1213. [CrossRef]
16. Alshammari, H.; El-Ghany, S.A.; Shehab, A. Big IoT Healthcare Data Analytics Framework Based on Fog and Cloud Computing. *J. Inf. Process. Syst.* **2020**, *16*, 1238–1249. [CrossRef]
17. Chen, R.C.; Saravanarajan, V.S.; Hung, H.T. Monitoring the Behaviours of Pet Cat Based on YOLO Model and Raspberry Pi. *Int. J. Appl. Sci. Eng.* **2021**, *18*, 1–12. [CrossRef]
18. Wutke, M.; Schmitt, A.O.; Traulsen, I.; Gültas, M. Investigation of Pig Activity Based on Video Data and Semi-Supervised Neural Networks. *AgriEngineering* **2020**, *2*, 581–595. [CrossRef]
19. Kearney, S.; Li, W.; Parsons, M.; Kim, K.I.; Cosker, D. RGBD-Dog: Predicting Canine Pose from RGBD Sensors. In Proceedings of the 2020 IEEE/CVF Conference on Computer Vision and Pattern Recognition (CVPR), Seattle, WA, USA, 16 June 2020; pp. 8333–8342.
20. Pereira, T.D.; Aldarondo, D.E.; Willmore, L.; Kislin, M.; Wang, S.S.H.; Murthy, M.; Shaevitz, J.W. Fast Animal Pose Estimation Using Deep Neural Networks. *Nat. Methods* **2019**, *16*, 117–125. [CrossRef]
21. Zamansky, A.; van der Linden, D.; Hadar, I.; Bleuer-Elsner, S. Log My Dog: Perceived Impact of Dog Activity Tracking. *Computer* **2019**, *52*, 35–43. [CrossRef]
22. van der Linden, D.; Zamansky, A.; Hadar, I.; Craggs, B.; Rashid, A. Buddy's Wearable Is Not Your Buddy: Privacy Implications of Pet Wearables. *IEEE Secur. Priv.* **2019**, *17*, 28–39. [CrossRef]
23. Aich, S.; Chakraborty, S.; Sim, J.S.; Jang, D.J.; Kim, H.C. The Design of an Automated System for the Analysis of the Activity and Emotional Patterns of Dogs with Wearable Sensors Using Machine Learning. *Appl. Sci.* **2019**, *9*, 4938. [CrossRef]
24. Ladha, C.; Hammerla, N.; Hughes, E.; Olivier, P.; Ploetz, T. Dog's Life: Wearable Activity Recognition for Dogs. In Proceedings of the 2013 ACM International Joint Conference on Pervasive and Ubiquitous Computing, Zurich, Switzerland, 8 September 2013; pp. 415–418.
25. Kumpulainen, P.; Cardó, A.V.; Somppi, S.; Törnqvist, H.; Väätäjä, H.; Majaranta, P.; Gizatdinova, Y.; Hoog Antink, C.; Surakka, V.; Kujala, M.V.; et al. Dog Behaviour Classification with Movement Sensors Placed on the Harness and the Collar. *Appl. Anim. Behav. Sci.* **2021**, *241*, 105393. [CrossRef]
26. Jo, Y.H.; Lee, H.J.; Kim, Y.H. Implementation of a Classification System for Dog Behaviors using YOLI-based Object Detection and a Node.js Server. *J. Inst. Converg. Signal Process.* **2020**, *21*, 29–37. [CrossRef]
27. Liu, Y.; Sun, P.; Wergeles, N.; Shang, Y. A Survey and Performance Evaluation of Deep Learning Methods for Small Object Detection. *Expert Syst. Appl.* **2021**, *172*, 114602. [CrossRef]

28. Nguyen, N.D.; Do, T.; Ngo, T.D.; Le, D.D. An Evaluation of Deep Learning Methods for Small Object Detection. *J. Electr. Comput. Eng.* **2020**, *2020*, 1–18. [CrossRef]
29. Bochkovskiy, A.; Wang, C.Y.; Liao, H.Y.M. YOLOv4: Optimal Speed and Accuracy of Object Detection. *arXiv* **2020**, arXiv:2004.10934.

Article

A Convolution Neural Network-Based Representative Spatio-Temporal Documents Classification for Big Text Data

Byoungwook Kim [1], Yeongwook Yang [2], Ji Su Park [3] and Hong-Jun Jang [3,*]

[1] Department of Computer Science and Engineering, Dongshin University, Naju 58245, Korea; bwkim@dsu.ac.kr
[2] Division of Computer Engineering, Hanshin University, Osan 18101, Korea; yeongwook.yang@hs.ac.kr
[3] Department of Computer Science and Engineering, Jeonju University, Jeonju 55069, Korea; jisupark@jj.ac.kr
* Correspondence: hongjunjang@jj.ac.kr; Tel.: +82-63-220-2372

Citation: Kim, B.; Yang, Y.; Park, J.S.; Jang, H.-J. A Convolution Neural Network-Based Representative Spatio-Temporal Documents Classification for Big Text Data. *Appl. Sci.* **2022**, *12*, 3843. https://doi.org/10.3390/app12083843

Academic Editors: Wei Wang and Ka Lok Man

Received: 20 January 2022
Accepted: 7 April 2022
Published: 11 April 2022

Publisher's Note: MDPI stays neutral with regard to jurisdictional claims in published maps and institutional affiliations.

Copyright: © 2022 by the authors. Licensee MDPI, Basel, Switzerland. This article is an open access article distributed under the terms and conditions of the Creative Commons Attribution (CC BY) license (https://creativecommons.org/licenses/by/4.0/).

Abstract: With the proliferation of mobile devices, the amount of social media users and online news articles are rapidly increasing, and text information online is accumulating as big data. As spatio-temporal information becomes more important, research on extracting spatiotemporal information from online text data and utilizing it for event analysis is being actively conducted. However, if spatiotemporal information that does not describe the core subject of a document is extracted, it is rather difficult to guarantee the accuracy of core event analysis. Therefore, it is important to extract spatiotemporal information that describes the core topic of a document. In this study, spatio-temporal information describing the core topic of a document is defined as 'representative spatio-temporal information', and documents containing representative spatiotemporal information are defined as 'representative spatio-temporal documents'. We proposed a character-level Convolution Neuron Network (CNN)-based document classifier to classify representative spatio-temporal documents. To train the proposed CNN model, 7400 training data were constructed for representative spatio-temporal documents. The experimental results show that the proposed CNN model outperforms traditional machine learning classifiers and existing CNN-based classifiers.

Keywords: convolution neural network; spatio-temporal document; document classification; big text data

1. Introduction

Since social media-based data or online media data is composed of natural language, it has a much larger and more complex structure than existing transaction data [1,2]. Recently, the media distributes news articles online in order to quickly deliver news to consumers, online news articles can identify current social trends and behavioral patterns of members of society [3]. The social trend analysis technology for content published in online media has the advantage of being less expensive and faster than the analysis by existing expert groups. Therefore, research to detect and monitor current major issues by analyzing unstructured text information from social media or online news posts and extracting useful knowledge is being actively conducted.

For social trend analysis, it is important to identify event sentences from text documents such as social media or online news articles [4]. The event sentence refers to a sentence in which specific content about a specific topic, i.e., who, where, when, what, what, etc. is expressed. The temporal and spatial information included in news articles is used to detect the early onset of disease and to determine the time and location of disease outbreaks [5]. The temporal and spatial information presented in online news articles plays a decisively important role in understanding social trends.

Existing research to detect spatial and temporal information from text focuses on how accurately all temporal and spatial information contained within a document is extracted [6–8]. A document can contain many pieces of information about time and space.

In this study, among various spatial and temporal information included in a document, temporal and spatial information describing the core topic of the document is defined as *'representative spatio-temporal information'*. The document including representative spatio-temporal information is defined as a *'representative spatiotemporal document'*. If not only representative spatio-temporal information but also a large number of general spatio-temporal information are extracted from one document, the accuracy of core event analysis based on spatio-temporal information can be lowered. In order to increase the accuracy of core event analysis through artificial intelligence, it is necessary to remove unnecessary spatio-temporal information from one document and extract only the representative spatio-temporal information that accurately describes the core event in the document. Since extracting representative spatio-temporal information from a single document is a high-cost task, it is difficult to treat all documents from big data such as social media-based data or online news articles as analysis targets. Therefore, in order to efficiently analyze core events through representative spatio-temporal information, it is important to select documents from which representative spatio-temporal information is extracted.

Research using machine learning (Naïve Bayes [9,10], SVM [11,12] and Random Forest [13,14], etc.) in automatic document classification problems have been conducted so far. Recently, as deep learning-based Convolution Neuron Network (CNN) has been used for document classification, the performance of automatic document classification has been greatly improved [15]. CNN started to attract attention in the field of artificial intelligence as it showed excellent performance in image classification or object detection in the early days [16–18]. Classification technology using CNN has expanded its field of application from images to texts [19]. Recently, document classification using CNN is characterized as an area that classifies documents (patent documents [20], contracts [21], infectious disease documents [22], etc.) of a specific domain.

In this paper, we propose a character-level CNN-based representative spatio-temporal document classification model. First, we built 7400 learning data from online news articles provided by the National Institute of the Korean Language [23]. We developed a character-level CNN-based document classifier (a.k.a. RepSTDoc_ConvNet) that can classify representative spatio-temporal documents. RepSTDoc_ConvNet has a deeper CNN layer and a fully-connected layer than the existing CNN-based document classification model. In order to prove the performance of the proposed CNN model, we compared RepSTDoc_ConvNet with three baseline machine learning classifiers (Gaussian Naïve Bayes, linear SVM, and random forest) and three deep learning-based models (ConvNet, DocClass_ConvNet [22] and DocClass_ConvNet_Mod).

The final goal of our study is to extract representative spatio-temporal information from a large amount of documents. In order to extract representative spatio-temporal information, it is first necessary to classify representative spatio-temporal documents having representative spatio-temporal information in a large number of documents. This paper corresponds to the stage of classification of representative spatio-temporal documents. Through the representative spatio-temporal information, it can be used for natural disaster detection and analysis of factors (events such as urban planning, building construction, traffic control, and store opening) influencing business district analysis.

Our main contributions are summarized as follows.

- We defined a novel problem of classifying representative spatio-temporal documents containing spatio-temporal information describing the core topic of a document.
- We developed 7400 learning data for representative spatio-temporal documents.
- We proposed a character-level CNN-based document classifier to classify representative spatio-temporal documents.
- The proposed RepSTDoc_ConvNet outperforms traditional machine learning classifiers, achieving the F1 score of 61.2%.

The rest of the paper is organized as follows. Section 2 presents the literature review. In Section 3, we define the research problem. Section 4 is the proposed CNN-based document classifier model. In Section 5, we provide the experimental results and discuss the detailed implications along with their results. Section 6 presents the conclusion.

2. Literature Reviews

2.1. Traditional Machine Learning-Based Document Classification

The study of classifying documents using machine learning rather than reading documents by humans and classifying them into a given class has been conducted using traditional machine learning. Among the various document classifications, the field of detecting whether or not spam is spam was treated as an initial document classification problem. The most common machine learning algorithms used to detect spam emails are Gaussian Naive Bayes, Support Vector Machines (SVMs), and Neural Networks. Gaussian Naive Bayes (GNB) is one of the earliest document classification algorithms applied to spam filtering because it has low false positives and simple processing [9,10]. GNB uses a conditional probability function combined with a simple bag-of-words feature to determine the overall probability of whether a given email is spam or not. First, stop words are deleted from the message, and the message is split into individual words. In all messages in the data set, the total frequency of occurrence for the entire list of words is calculated. A threshold is applied to delete the least frequent words and complete the unique vocabulary of the data. The spam or non-spam label is then used to calculate the probability of each word being included in the spam message. Finally, the probability that the message is spam is calculated by combining the spam probability of each word in the message. Mitra et al. [24] present a least-squares support vector machine (LS-SVM) that classifies noisy document titles into various predetermined categories. Random Forest (RF) classifiers are suitable for text classification on high-dimensional noise data. Islam et al. [25] proposed a dynamic ensemble selection method to improve the performance of a random forest classifier in text classification.

2.2. Deep Learning-Based Document Classification

Deep learning uses multi-layered artificial neural networks and learns useful features directly from data. Deep learning is changing the paradigm of machine learning research, showing remarkable performance gains in many areas of computer vision. Deep learning technology has been applied to computer vision since 1989, and Yann LeCun [26] proposed a Convolutional Neural Network that divides an image into several local regions and shares weights for character recognition in an automatic postal classification system. CNN learns features of input data using tensors as input, passes the data through a layer of neurons that classifies the data into multiple stages, and computes the weights to pass as input to the next layer. The main components that make CNN different from neural networks are three layers (convolutional layer, pooling layer, and fully connected layer). The convolutional layer convolves the multidimensional features of the input tensor and outputs a reduced vectorization to pass to the pooling layer. In the max-pooling layer, we extract the maxima from each neuron cluster in the previous layer, reducing the dimensionality while retaining important information from the convolution. The final fully connected layer connects the final node to each specified output class. Recently, in the field of computer vision, a Recurrent Neural Network (RNN) is being used for image and video description generation, handwriting recognition, and text or sound translation functions in images or videos [27].

Deep learning is being actively applied not only to computer vision but also to text classification which identifies what kind of category the input text belongs to. Word2Vec is used to transform the text into tensors or vectorized representations for processing in CNNs. CNN showed higher performance in spam classification than traditional machine learning methods. Huang [28] proposed a CNN (Convolutional Neural Network) model for Chinese SMS (Short Message Service) spam detection. This study also discusses the influence of hyper-parameters on CNN models and proposes optimal combinations of hyper-parameters. Liu et al. [29] proposed a modified deep CNN model for email sentiment classification. Mutabazi et al. [30] provided reviews of various medical text question-answering systems using deep learning. Kim et al. [22] developed a document classification model related to infectious diseases using deep learning. A document classification model was constructed using two deep learning algorithms (ConvNet and BiLSTM) and two classification methods, DocClass and SenClass. Given a specific text extraction system, it was shown to be compatible with the classification performance of human experts. It has shown the potential of using deep learning to identify epidemic outbreaks.

Table 1 presents the summary of methods for text classification.

Table 1. Summary of methods for text classification.

Methods.	Technique
Gaussian Naive Bayes [9,10]	Gaussian Naive Bayes is used for text classification based on Bayes theorem under a normal distribution with sample mean and sample variance.
Linear SVM [11,12,24]	When a set of data belonging to one of two categories is given, SVMs are powerful machine learning supervised learning models that can be used for classification tasks.
Random Forest [13,14,25]	Random forest is an ensemble method for learning multiple decision trees. Random forests are being used for various problems such as detection, classification, and regression.
ConvNet [15]	CNN is a type of multi-layer feed-forward artificial neural network. It is a deep neural network technology that can process regional features of data by applying filtering techniques to artificial neural networks.

3. Problem

In this section, we first define several concepts as well as the problem of representative spatio-temporal documents.

Subject of the document. Let $D = \{d_1, \ldots, d_n\}$ be a set of documents. Each document has a core subject, which is the message the author wants to convey to the reader. For example, consider a news article reporting the damage of a typhoon that occurred on Jeju Island, South Korea on September 7. $d_i.subject$ = {'typhoon damage'} denotes the subject of d_i is about the damage caused by the typhoon that occurred on Jeju Island on September 7.

Spatio-temporal word. $d_i = \{s_1, \ldots, s_m\}$ is a sequence of sentences and $s_i = \{w_1, \ldots, w_l\}$ is a sequence of words. Among the words contained in a document, there are words for a specific time and place where an event occurred. $w_i.time$ = {'September 7'} denotes that an event occurred on September 7. $w_j.place$ = {'Jeju Island'} denotes that the place where an event occurred is Jeju Island.

Representativeness of spatio-temporal word. Several spatio-temporal words can exist in one document. Some of the spatio-temporal words are related to the subject of the document, and some are not. Among spatio-temporal words, we consider the words most relevant to the subject of a document as 'representative spatio-temporal words'. We denote a representative spatio-temporal word, $w_i.presentativeness = true$.

Representative spatio-temporal document. We define a document containing both a representative spatial word and a representative temporal word among words included in one document as a representative spatio-temporal document.

4. Materials and Methods

4.1. Datasets

In this study, learning data for the classification of representative spatio-temporal documents were constructed using the published Korean corpus. The National Institute of Korean Language [23] discloses various data in Korean. In this study, a newspaper corpus provided by the National Institute of the Korean Language for research purposes was used to construct learning data for representative spatio-temporal documents. The newspaper corpus provided by the National Institute of the Korean Language is a collection of newspaper articles produced for 10 years from 2009 to 2018 with a total of 3,536,491 articles.

The corpus consists of a total of 363 files, with a total size of 15.6 GB. The original file is composed of JSON (UTF-8 encoding). Raw data contains article content in the document tag. One article consists of a metadata tag indicating the metadata of the article (title, article name, newspaper company, publication date, and subject) and a paragraph tag indicating the article body. In the paragraph, the article body is divided into paragraphs and composed of form tags.

4.2. Data Preprocessing

We constructed representative spatio-temporal information learning data for 7400 articles out of 3,536,491 articles. Eight workers read the content of the news article and judge whether the article has representative spatio-temporal information. In order to improve the performance of artificial intelligence systems, the quality of training data is important. In order to maintain the consistency of data quality among workers, we cross-checked each other's work results three times.

4.3. Deep Learning Model

Determining whether or not a news article is a representative spatiotemporal document is a binary classification problem. We used a deep learning neural network model, a character-level convolutional neural network (CNN) called ConvNet [15]. In general, ConvNet divides sentences/paragraphs/documents into word unit tokens when text classification is performed. However, Zhang et al. [15] argue that by using the character (alphabetic) unit instead of the word unit token, a good enough performance for the Natural Language Processing (NLP) task can be achieved without using the word unit. An attempt to use tokening as a character-level unit was first presented in this paper. We also used an embedding matrix created by tokenizing the text in character units as shown in Figure 1.

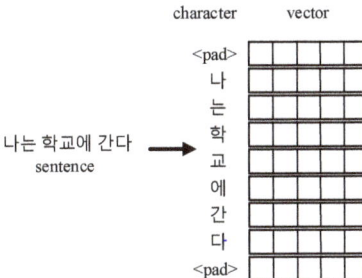

Figure 1. Character-level embedding. ('나는 학교에 간다' in Korean means 'I go to school' in English).

ConvNet treats each document as a series of characters and is passed to 6 convolutional and max-pooling layers and 3 fully connected layers to determine the probability that a document belongs to a positive class. Because this model does not require pre-trained embedded words, it learns quickly and with reasonable performance compared to word-level models.

We developed a character-level CNN-based document classifier to classify representative spatio-temporal documents, RepSTDoc_ConvNet using the entire document as input. We used the layers of the CNN model, DocClass_ConvNet, in [22] as our baseline. Figure 2 shows a comparison of the two models.

ConvNet has both 9 layers deep with 6 convolutional layers and 3 fully-connected layers. DocClass_ConvNet has both 6 layers deep with 4 convolutional layers and 2 fully-connected layers. RepSTDoc_ConvNet has both 12 layers deep with 9 convolutional layers and 3 fully-connected layers.

In order to train a ConvNet model, we need to keep documents of various lengths constant. Considering the hardware memory constraint and the length distribution of the training data, the number of characters in the document was set to 4700 in ConvNet. Long text is truncated and short text is padded.

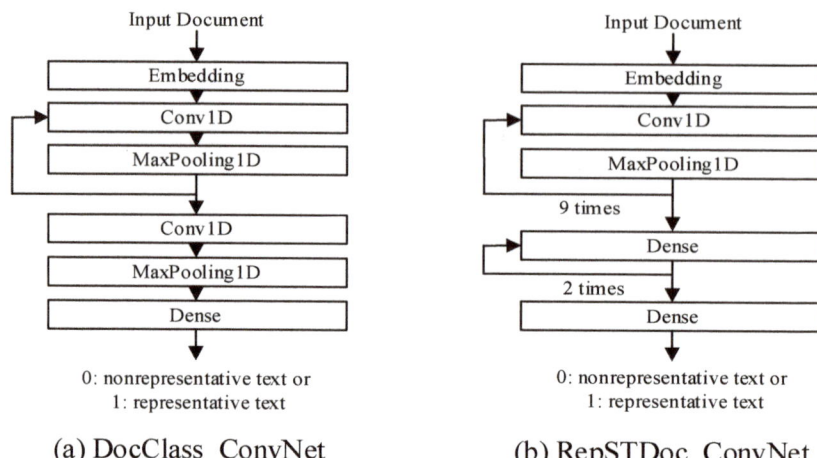

Figure 2. A comparison of DocClass_ConvNet [22] and RepSTDoc ConvNet.

5. Result and Discussion

In this section, we present comprehensive experimental results of the deep learning model. The purpose of this paper is to develop a classifier for representative spatio-temporal documents based on deep learning. To evaluate the performance of a proposed deep learning-based classifier, we first evaluated the performance of three traditional machine learning algorithms: Gaussian Naïve Bayes, Linear SVM, and Random Forest. For performance comparison with our CNN model (RepSTDoc_ConvNet), we also evaluated the performance of DocClass_ConvNet, an existing CNN-based document binary classifier, and DocClass_ConvNet_Mod, which adjusted hyper-parameters in the DocClass_ConvNet model to fit our dataset.

To confirm that our CNN model works properly, we pre-tested the performance of binary classification using the benchmark spam dataset from the UCI Repository [31]. The spam dataset contained 5572 messages in English. This spam dataset was fed to our proposed CNN model and the experimental results were as follows: accuracy (0.982), precision (0.962), recall (0.916), and F1-score (0.938). This result is not significantly different from that of the recently published CNN model [32].

All experiments were carried out on conducted on a GeForce RTX 2080 Ti 11GB GPU and an Intel(R) Xeon CPU with 64 GB memory.

5.1. Performance Evaluation

For the experiment, we divided the collected data into training (60%), validation (20%), and test data (20%) as shown in Table 2. Target data were distributed to each data about 25.23%. The training data was used to train the model, the validation data was used to select the best performing model in the training process, and the test set was used to evaluate the performance of the finally selected model.

Table 2. Statistics of training, validation, and test data.

Split Data	Count	Non RepSTDoc	RepSTDoc	Ratio
Training	4440	3319	1121	25.25%
Validation	1480	1107	373	25.20%
Test	1480	1107	373	25.20%
Total	7400	5533	1867	25.23%

5.2. Hyper-Parameter Tuning

CNN consists of several hyper-parameters such as kernel size, batch size, dropout rate, learning rate, pooling window size, pooling type, activation function, number of neurons in a density layer, and optimization function, etc. We found the most suitable parameter values for the proposed model by manually adjusting the values of each parameter. We found the optimal parameter values by using the learning curves for accuracy and loss of training data and validation data for every experiment. We set up the experimental environment with various parameters, the parameters used in the experiment are summarized in Table 3, and the parameter values with the highest performance are shown in bold. During the training process of the CNN model, we trained our CNN model with up to 1000 epochs and early stopping patience = 220.

Table 3. Hyper-parameters for the experiments.

Hyper-Parameter	Values
Kernel size	2, 3, 4, **5**, 6, 7
Feature maps	32. 64, 128, **256**, 512
Pooling window size	**3**, 4, 5
Pooling type	Max pooling
Activation function	ReLu
Dense layer neurons	**100**, 300
Dropout rate	0.3, 0.4, 0.5, **0.6**, 0.7, 0.8
Batch size	16, 32, **64**, 128, 256
Learning rate	0.1, 0.01, 0.001, 0.0001, **0.00001**, 0.000001
Optimizer	**Adam**, RMSprop

Overfitting deep learning models makes it difficult to trust their predictive performance on new data. Therefore, training should be stopped when the loss in the validation data is no longer reduced during the training phase. Early stopping is one of the regularization techniques that makes neural networks avoid overfitting [33]. We can use the EarlyStopping callback to terminate the model early when the performance index of the model does not improve during the set epoch. Through a combination of EarlyStopping and ModelCheckpoint callbacks, it is possible to trigger an early shutdown for non-improving training and resume training by reloading the best model from ModelCheckpoint. Both training loss and validation loss decrease until overfitting occur, but when overfitting occurs, training loss decreases while validation loss increases. Thus, we set the monitor option of EarlyStopping callback to stop training when the validation loss increases.

5.3. Experimental Results

We compared the RepSTDoc_ConvNet with three baseline machine learning classifiers (Gaussian naïve Bayes, linear SVM, and random forest) and three deep learning models (ConvNet, DocClass_ConvNet, and DocClass_ConvNet_Mod). DocClass_ConvNet is a model in which the CNN layer and hyper-parameters presented in the study are identical. DocClass_ConvNet_Mod is a model that optimizes the hyper-parameter values according to the experimental data while maintaining the same CNN layer of DocClass_ConvNet. Deep learning includes the process of randomly setting weight values during model training. Therefore, to compensate for such randomness, the average performance was measured after performing each experiment 10 times. The experimental results are presented in Table 4.

The accuracy of machine learning algorithms to classify representative spatio-temporal documents was derived from a minimum of 0.74 to a maximum of 0.79. This accuracy is far below the performance of machine learning that deals with general document classification problems. The CNN layer used in this paper derives relatively high performance in the spam classification problem. From these results, it can be seen that classifying representative spatio-temporal documents is a difficult problem.

Table 4. Comparison of evaluation based on the precision, recall, F1 score, and accuracy.

Machine Learning	Precision	Recall	F1 score	Accuracy
Gaussian Naïve Bayes	0.562	0.224	0.320	0.751
Linear SVM	0.626	0.421	0.503	0.783
Random Forest	**0.729**	0.191	0.303	0.770
ConvNet	0.525	0.591	0.556	0.762
DocClass_ConvNet	0.511	0.453	0.480	0.744
DocClass_ConvNet_Mod	0.614	0.496	0.548	**0.794**
RepSTDoc_ConvNet	0.552	**0.673**	**0.612**	0.785

Random Forest showed the highest precision with 0.729 and DocClass_ConvNet_Mod showed the highest accuracy with 0.794. RepSTDoc_ConvNet showed the highest recall and F1-score with 0.673 and 0.612, respectively. In terms of accuracy, DocClass_ConvNet_Mod seems to have the highest performance with 0.794. However, considering the confusion matrix, it does not seem appropriate to evaluate the performance of machine learning only with accuracy in the problem of classifying representative spatio-temporal documents. Figure 3 shows three confusion matrixes of Linear SVM, Random Forest, and RepSTDoc_ConvNet.

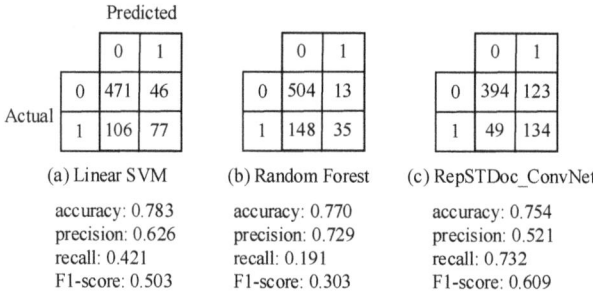

(a) Linear SVM
accuracy: 0.783
precision: 0.626
recall: 0.421
F1-score: 0.503

(b) Random Forest
accuracy: 0.770
precision: 0.729
recall: 0.191
F1-score: 0.303

(c) RepSTDoc_ConvNet
accuracy: 0.754
precision: 0.521
recall: 0.732
F1-score: 0.609

Figure 3. Comparison of confusion matrixes (**a**) Linear SVM, (**b**) Random Forest, and (**c**) RepSTDoc_ConvNet. '0' means the nonrepresentative spatio-temporal document and '1' means the representative spatio-temporal document.

In the validation data used to evaluate the proposed CNN model, the proportion of representative spatio-temporal documents (RepSTDoc) is only 25.20%. Therefore, even when the model is not trained at all, the accuracy is 74.80%. In this case, high accuracy is maintained even if the number of documents predicted by the model with RepSTDoc is small. In Figure 3a, Linear SVM classified 123 documents (46 false positives, 77 true positive) as RepSTDoc. Even if the model training is not done properly, the high true negative value (471) results in high accuracy. A random forest with the second-highest accuracy is also similar to Linear SVM. In the random forest, the accuracy is 0.770 even though there are few documents classified by RepSTDoc (48) because the model is hardly trained. The fact that the number of documents predicted as RepSTDoc is small because the model is not trained can be confirmed by the small recall value (0.191). In Figure 3c, RepSTDoc_ConvNet classified 257 documents (123 false positives, 134 true positive) as RepSTDoc. In RepSTDoc_ConvNet, as the value of true positive increased, the value of false-positive also increased. The fact that the model classified many documents as RepSTDoc can be seen from the high value of recall (0.609). This phenomenon occurs because the number of positive and false documents in the data is imbalanced. Therefore, in order to accurately evaluate the performance of the model, the F1-score, which considers both precision and recall, should be used as a measure. In terms of the F1-score, RepSTDoc_ConvNet yields the highest performance with 0.609.

We measured the classification accuracy of human workers on 1400 learning data to verify the challenge of the representative spatio-temporal document classification problem. The 1400 learning data consists of 359 representative spatio-temporal documents and 1041 non-representative spatio-temporal documents. Four workers who participated in building learning data classified representative spatio-temporal documents for 1400 learning data. For each learning data, the number of workers who judged actual representative spatio-temporal documents as representative spatio-temporal documents (True Positive: TP) and the number of workers who judged non-representative spatio-temporal documents (False Negative: FN) were calculated.

For one actual representative spatio-temporal document, the ratio was calculated by dividing the number of all four people judged as TP, the number of three or more judged as TP, the number of two or more judged as TP, and the number of one or more judged as TP in Table 5. For each of the 359 representative spatiotemporal documents, the number of documents judged as TP by all 4 people was 189 (52.64%), the number of documents judged as TP by 3 or more people 251 (69.92%), and the number of documents judged as TP by 2 or more people was 310 (89.35%), the number of documents judged as TP by 1 or more people was 332 (92.48%).

Table 5. The ratio and count of actual representative spatio-temporal documents to be judged as representative spatio-temporal documents according to workers.

	4	>3	>2	>1
ratio	52.64%	69.91%	86.35%	92.47%
count	189	251	310	332

For one actual nonrepresentative spatio-temporal document, the ratio was also calculated by dividing the number of all 4 people judged as FN, the number of 3 or more people judged as FN, the number of 2 or more people judged as FN, and the number of 1 or more people judged as FN in Table 6. For each of the 1041 nonrepresentative spatio-temporal documents, the number of documents judged as FN by all 4 people was 5 (0.48%), the number of documents judged as FN by 3 or more people was 24 (2.31%), and the number of documents judge as FN by 2 or more people (6.34%), and the number of documents judged as FN by more than one person was 135 (12.97%).

Table 6. The ratio and count of actual nonrepresentative spatio-temporal documents to be judged as nonrepresentative spatio-temporal documents according to workers.

	4	>3	>2	>1
ratio	0.48%	2.30%	6.34%	12.96%
count	5	24	66	135

First of all, we describe the challenge of the representative spatio-temporal document classification problem through the ratio of documents in which at least three people, more than half of the judges, judged the actual representative spatio-temporal document as the representative spatio-temporal document. About 70% of the three or more people judged the actual representative spatio-temporal document as TP, and the ratio of all four people who judged it as TP was only about 53%, confirming that it is difficult for humans to classify representative spatio-temporal documents from large documents.

5.4. Effect of Learning Rate

The learning rate refers to the amount by which the weights are updated during model training and determines how quickly the model adapts to the problem. Larger learning rates converge more quickly to suboptimal solutions, while lower learning rates can result in early intervening learning. One of the important hyper-parameters that must be appropriately selected in deep learning neural network model training is the learning rate. We experimented with the effect of learning rate [0.1, 0.01, 0.001, 0.0001, 0.00001, 0.000001] on performance.

Figure 4 shows the effect of the learning rate for ConvNet, DocClass_ConvNet_Mod, and RepSTDoc_ConvNet. The learning rate at which no training was performed in each model was not shown on the graph (learning rate: 0.1, 0.01, and 0.000001). In the section where the model is trained, the F1-score tends to increase as the learning rate decreases. There is a large difference in performance according to the learning rate in each model. In the representative spatio-temporal learning data used in this study, the learning rate shows the highest performance at 0.00001.

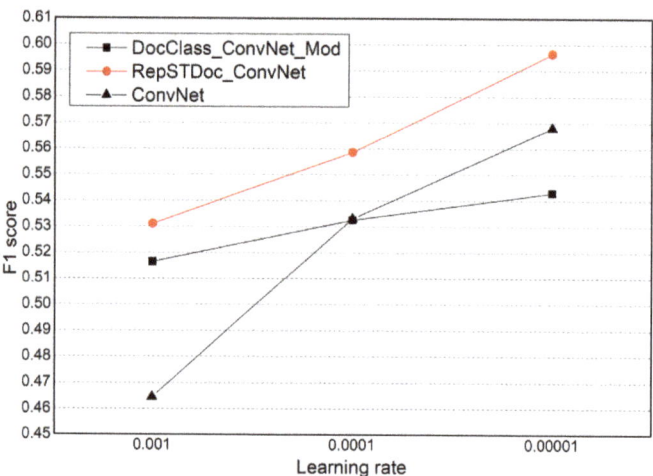

Figure 4. The effect of learning rate.

5.5. Effect of Batch Size

Most of the training of deep learning models is based on mini-batch stochastic gradient descent (SGD). At this time, the batch size is one of the important hyper-parameters when training the actual model. Various studies are being conducted regarding the effect of the batch size on model training. Although it has not been clearly identified yet, it is experimentally observed in several studies that the use of a small batch size has a positive effect on generalization performance. We experimented with the effect of learning rate [16, 32, 64, 128, and 256] on performance.

Figure 5 shows the effect of batch size for ConvNet, DocClass_ConvNet_Mod, and RepSTDoc_ConvNet. In the representative spatio-temporal learning data used in this study, there was no consistent performance variability across models. RepSTDoc_ConvNet shows a tendency to improve performance as the batch size increases in the model training section [32, 64, 128, and 256]. However, in DocClass_ConvNet_Mod, the variation of performance according to the batch size was not consistent. Although this result cannot be generalized, the batch size may not affect the performance of the model depending on the complexity of the CNN layer and the characteristics of the data.

5.6. Time Efficiency

The numbers of weights are 1,410,609, 1,446,261, and 5,083,129 in DocClass_ConvNet_Mod, ConvNet and RepSTDoc_ConvNet respectively. The overall algorithm time is affected by the complexity of the neural network. This is because the amount of computation increases as the number of weights in the network increases. Table 7 shows the time efficiencies for the three algorithms.

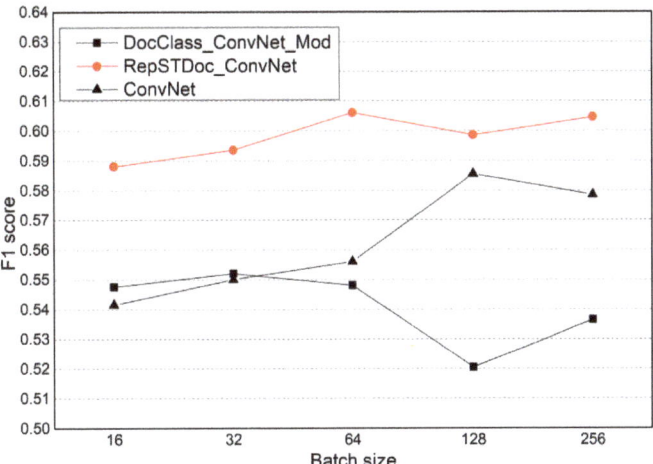

Figure 5. The effect of batch size.

Table 7. The comparison of the time.

Methods	Avg. Epoch	Avg. Time (s)	Avg. Time per Epoch (s)
ConvNet	405	387	0.912
DocClass_ConvNet_Mod	398	332	0.849
RepSTDoc_ConvNet	687	903	1.313

5.7. Data Distribution Rate

We also investigated the performance difference according to the change in the distribution ratio of training, validation, and test data. The ratio of training data was set while keeping the ratio of validation data and test data the same. The distribution ratio used in the experiment is as follows: training, validation, and test data are 4:3:3, 6:2:2, and 8:1:1 respectively. Figure 6 shows the highest performance with a 6:2:2 distribution ratio. There is not much difference in the performance of each model according to the distribution ratio.

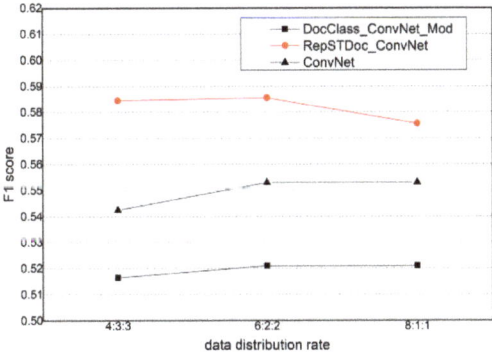

Figure 6. The effect of distribution rate.

5.8. Receiver Operating Characteristic

The Receiver Operating Characteristic (ROC) curve shows the performance of the binary classifier for various thresholds. Figure 7 shows the corresponding ROC curves when using ConvNet, DocClass_ConvNet_Mod, and RepSTDoc_ConvNet. ConvNet outperformed the other models in the lower-left corner. However, in the section where the false positive rate is greater than 0.2, RepSTDoc_ConvNet was superior to other models. RepSTDoc_ConvNet was found to have the best performance for classifying representative spatiotemporal documents.

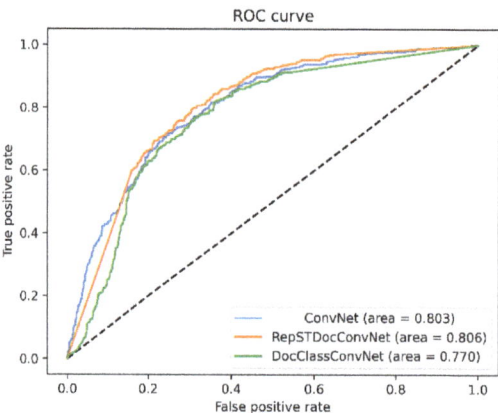

Figure 7. Receiver operating characteristic (ROC) curves of models classifying representative spatio-temporal documents using ConvNet, DocClass_ConvNet_Mod and RepSTDoc_ConvNet.

6. Conclusions

The purpose of this paper is to develop a CNN-based representative spatio-temporal document classification model. Because the representative spatio-temporal document is a novel concept, we defined a representative spatio-temporal document as documents containing spatio-temporal information describing the core topic of a document. We built 7400 learning data to train a CNN-based representative spatio-temporal document classifier and developed a character-level CNN-based document classifier to classify representative spatio-temporal documents. To evaluate the performance of RepSTDoc_ConvNet, we evaluated the performance of three traditional machine learning algorithms: Gaussian Naïve Bayes, Linear SVM, and Random Forest. For performance comparison with our RepSTDoc_ConvNet, we also evaluated the performance of ConvNet, DocClass_ConvNet, and DocClass_ConvNet_Mod. The experimental results show that RepSTDoc_ConvNet outperforms traditional machine learning classifiers and existing CNN-based classifiers.

A limitation of the work is that RepSTDoc_ConvNet still has lower performance compared to general document classifiers. It is necessary to diversify the features of the input data as it shows that classifying representative spatio-temporal documents is a difficult problem. In order to further improve the performance of the representative spatio-temporal document classifier, it is necessary to find a way to lower the false positive value by finding the characteristic that distinguishes the general spatio-temporal document from the representative spatio-temporal document.

Author Contributions: Conceptualization, H.-J.J. and B.K.; methodology, B.K.; software, B.K.; validation, H.-J.J.; investigation, Y.Y.; data curation, Y.Y. and B.K.; writing—original draft preparation, H.-J.J. and B.K.; writing—review and editing, J.S.P.; visualization, J.S.P.; supervision, B.K.; project administration, B.K.; funding acquisition, B.K. All authors have read and agreed to the published version of the manuscript.

Funding: This research was funded by the Basic Science Research Program through the National Research Foundation of Korea (NRF) funded by the Korean Government (MSIT) (No. 2021R1F1A1049387) and by industry-academic Cooperation R&D program funded by LX Spatial Information Research Institute (LXSIRI, Republic of Korea) [Project Name: A Study on the Establishment of Service Pipe Database for Safety Management of Underground Space/Project Number: 2021-502]. This result was supported by the "Regional Innovation Strategy (RIS)" through the National Research Foundation of Korea (NRF) funded by the Ministry of Education (MOE) (1345341782).

Institutional Review Board Statement: Not applicable.

Informed Consent Statement: Written informed consent has been obtained from the patient(s) to publish this paper.

Conflicts of Interest: The authors declare no conflict of interest.

References

1. Chew, A.M.K.; Gunasekeran, D.V. Social Media Big Data: The Good, The Bad, and the Ugly (Un)truths. *Front. Big Data* **2021**, *4*, 6. [CrossRef] [PubMed]
2. Nurdin, N. Research in Online Space: The Use of Social Media for Research Setting. *J. Inf. Syst.* **2017**, *13*, 67–77. [CrossRef]
3. Kim, M.; Newth, D.; Christen, P. Trends of news diffusion in social media based on crowd phenomena. In Proceedings of the Companion Publication of the 23rd International Conference on World Wide Web Companion, Seoul, Korea, 7–14 April 2014; International World Wide Web Conference Steering Committee: Geneva, Switzerland, 2014; pp. 753–758. [CrossRef]
4. Naughton, M.; Stokes, N.; Carthy, J. Sentence-level event classification in unstructured texts. *Inf. Retr.* **2010**, *13*, 132–156. [CrossRef]
5. Lan, R.; Adelfio, M.D.; Samet, H. Spatio-temporal disease tracking using news articles. In Proceedings of the HealthGIS'14: 3rd ACM SIGSPATIAL International Workshop on the Use of GIS in Public Health, Dallas, TX, USA, 4–7 November 2014; pp. 31–38. [CrossRef]
6. Badia, A.; Ravishankar, J.; Muezzinoglu, T. Text Extraction of Spatial and Temporal Information. In Proceedings of the 2007 IEEE Intelligence and Security Informatics, New Brunswick, NJ, USA, 23–24 May 2007. [CrossRef]
7. Lim, C.-G.; Jeong, Y.-S.; Choi, H.-J. Survey of Temporal Information Extraction. *J. Inf. Processing Syst.* **2019**, *15*, 931–956. [CrossRef]
8. Feriel, A.; Kholladi, M.-K. Automatic Extraction of Spatio-Temporal Information from Arabic Text Documents. *Int. J. Comput. Sci. Inf. Technol.* **2015**, *7*, 97–107. [CrossRef]
9. Chen, J.; Huang, H.; Tian, S.; Qu, Y. Feature selection for text classification with Naïve Bayes. *Expert Syst. Appl.* **2009**, *36*, 5432–5435. [CrossRef]
10. Pavel, H. How to Build and Apply Naive Bayes Classification for Spam Filtering. *Medium, Towards Data Science*, 31 January 2020.
11. Bedi, G. Simple Guide to Text Classification (NLP) Using SVM and Naive Bayes with Python. *Medium*, 13 July 2020.
12. Ray, S. SVM: Support Vector Machine Algorithm in Machine Learning. *Analytics Vidhya*, 23 December 2020.
13. Liparas, D.; HaCohen-Kerner, Y.; Moumtzidou, A.; Vrochidis, S.; Kompatsiaris, I. News Articles Classification Using Random Forests and Weighted Multimodal Features. In *Multidisciplinary Information Retrieval*; Springer: Cham, Switzerland, 2014; pp. 63–75. [CrossRef]
14. Sharma, S.K.; Sharma, N.K.; Potter, P.P. Fusion Approach for Document Classification using Random Forest and SVM. In Proceedings of the 9th International Conference System Modeling and Advancement in Research Trends (SMART), Moradabad, India, 4–5 December 2020. [CrossRef]
15. Zhang, X.; Zhao, J.; Yan, L.C. Character-Level Convolutional Networks for Text Classification. *arXiv* **2015**, arXiv:1509.01626.
16. Bibi, S.; Abbasi, A.; Haq, I.U.; Baik, S.W.; Ullah, A. Digital Image Forgery Detection Using Deep Autoencoder and CNN Features. *Hum. Cent. Comput. Inf. Sci.* **2021**, *11*, 1–17.
17. Song, W.; Zhang, L.; Tian, Y.; Fong, S.; Liu, J.; Gozho, A. CNN-based 3D object classification using Hough space of LiDAR point clouds. *Hum. Cent. Comput. Inf. Sci.* **2020**, *10*, 1–14. [CrossRef]
18. Song, W.; Liu, Z.; Tian, Y.; Fong, S. Pointwise CNN for 3D Object Classification on Point Cloud. *J. Inf. Proc. Syst.* **2021**, *17*, 787–800. [CrossRef]
19. Zeng, Y.; Zhang, R.; Yang, L.; Song, S. Cross-Domain Text Sentiment Classification Method Based on the CNN-BiLSTM-TE Model. *J. Inf. Proc. Syst.* **2021**, *17*, 818–833. [CrossRef]
20. Li, S.; Hu, J.; Cui, Y.; Hu, J. DeepPatent: Patent classification with convolutional neural networks and word embedding. *Scientometrics* **2018**, *117*, 721–744. [CrossRef]
21. Chen, Y.; Dai, H.; Yu, X.; Hu, W.; Xie, Z.; Tan, C. Improving Ponzi Scheme Contract Detection Using Multi-Channel TextCNN and Transformer. *Sensors* **2021**, *21*, 6417. [CrossRef] [PubMed]
22. Kim, M.; Chae, K.; Lee, S.; Jang, H.-J.; Kim, S. Automated Classification of Online Sources for Infectious Disease Occurrences Using Machine-Learning-Based Natural Language Processing Approaches. *Int. J. Environ. Res. Public Health* **2020**, *17*, 9467. [CrossRef] [PubMed]
23. National Institute of Korean Language [Internet]. Available online: https://www.korean.go.kr (accessed on 6 April 2022).
24. Mitra, V.; Wang, C.-J.; Banerjee, S. Text classification: A least square support vector machine approach. *Appl. Soft Comput.* **2007**, *7*, 908–914. [CrossRef]
25. Islam, M.Z.; Liu, J.; Li, J.; Liu, L.; Kang, W. A Semantics Aware Random Forest for Text Classification. In Proceedings of the 28th ACM International Conference on Information and Knowledge Management, CIKM'19, Beijing, China, 3–7 November 2019; pp. 1061–1070. [CrossRef]

26. LeCun, Y.; Bengio, Y.; Hinton, G. Deep learning. *Nature* **2015**, *521*, 436–444. [CrossRef] [PubMed]
27. Zhong, Z.; Gao, Y.; Zheng, Y.; Zheng, B. Efficient Spatio-Temporal Recurrent Neural Network for Video Deblurring. In *Computer Vision—ECCV 2020*; Vedaldi, A., Bischof, H., Brox, T., Frahm, J.M., Eds.; ECCV 2020. Lecture Notes in Computer Science; Springer: Cham, Switzerland, 2020; Volume 12351. [CrossRef]
28. Huang, T. A CNN Model for SMS Spam Detection. In Proceedings of the 4th International Conference on Mechanical, Control and Computer Engineering (ICMCCE), Hohhot, China, 25–27 October 2019.
29. Liu, S.; Lee, I. Sequence encoding incorporated CNN model for Email document sentiment classification. *Appl. Soft Comput. J.* **2021**, *102*, 107104. [CrossRef]
30. Mutabazi, E.; Ni, J.; Tang, G.; Cao, W. A Review on Medical Textual Question Answering Systems Based on Deep Learning Approaches. *Appl. Sci.* **2021**, *11*, 5456. [CrossRef]
31. Almeida, T.A.; Hidalgo, J.M.G.; Yamakami, A. Contributions to the study of sms spam filtering: New collection and results. In Proceedings of the 11th ACM Symposium on Document Engineering, Mountain View, CA, USA, 19–22 September 2011; pp. 259–262.
32. Roy, P.K.; Singh, J.P.; Banerjee, S. Deep learning to filter SMS Spam. *Future Gener. Comp. Syst.* **2019**, *102*, 524–533. [CrossRef]
33. Goodfellow, I.; Yoshua, B.; Courville, A. *Deep Learning*; MIT Press: Cambridge, MA, USA, 2016.

Article

A Smart-Mutual Decentralized System for Long-Term Care

Hsien-Ming Chou

Department of Information Management, Chung Yuan Christian University, Taoyuan City 32023, Taiwan; chou0109@cycu.edu.tw

Abstract: Existing caretakers of long-term care are assigned constrainedly and randomly to taking care of older people, which could lead to issues of shortage of manpower and poor human quality, especially the proportion of older people increases year after year to let long-term care become more and more important. In addition, due to different backgrounds, inadequate caregivers may cause older people to suffer from spiritual alienation under the current system. Most of the existing studies present a centralized architecture, but even if technology elements are incorporated, such as cloud center services or expert systems, it is still impossible to solve the above-mentioned challenges. This study moves past the centralized architecture and attempts to use the decentralized architecture with Artificial Intelligence and Blockchain technology to refine the model of providing comprehensive care for older people. Using the proposed mapping mutual clustering algorithm in this study, the positions of caregivers and older people can be changed at any time based on the four main background elements: risk level, physiology, medical record, and demography. In addition, this study uses the proposed long-term care decentralized architecture algorithm to solve the stability of care records with transparency to achieve the effect of continuous tracking. Based on previous records, it can also dynamically change the new matching mode. The main contribution of this research is the proposal of an innovative solution to the problem of mental alienation, insufficient manpower, and the privacy issue. In addition, this study evaluates the proposed method through practical experiments. The corporation features have been offered and evaluated with user perceptions by a one-sample t-test; the proposed algorithm to the research model also has been compared with not putting it into the model through ANOVA analysis to get that all hypotheses are supported. The results reveal a high level of accuracy of the proposed mutual algorithm forecasting and positive user perceptions from the post-study questionnaire. As an emerging research topic, this study undoubtedly provides an important research basis for scholars and experts who are interested in continued related research in the future.

Keywords: older people; long-term care; artificial intelligence; blockchain technology; decentralized architecture

Citation: Chou, H.-M. A Smart-Mutual Decentralized System for Long-Term Care. *Appl. Sci.* **2022**, *12*, 3664. https://doi.org/10.3390/app12073664

Academic Editors: Wei Wang and Ka Lok Man

Received: 16 March 2022
Accepted: 3 April 2022
Published: 6 April 2022

Publisher's Note: MDPI stays neutral with regard to jurisdictional claims in published maps and institutional affiliations.

Copyright: © 2022 by the author. Licensee MDPI, Basel, Switzerland. This article is an open access article distributed under the terms and conditions of the Creative Commons Attribution (CC BY) license (https://creativecommons.org/licenses/by/4.0/).

1. Introduction

Older people normally manage their daily activities in residential aged care through family members, professional caregivers, or by themselves. However, most care agencies focused on the cost of employees and always have a lack of staff, leading to limitations on the healthcare systems [1,2]. In addition, differences in backgrounds between the generations can cause generation gap issues such as different ideas, education, and even political leanings [3,4]. The current method of human resources distribution, as assigned by care agencies, is insufficient because older people are participants in different social networks. In particular, the COVID-19 pandemic has made these long-term care facilities with staff much riskier than dynamic mutual ways to keep sufficient caretakers [5,6]. Older people interact with others on managing spiritual loneliness and watching out for accidents. Older people are often highly active, unlike those in nursing care with chronic diseases, so it is necessary to consider their willingness to collaborate. In the past, long-term care homes with social connections keep stable caretakers and well relationships among long-term care residents. However, from this traditional center architecture aspect to protect people living in long-term care from COVID-19 infection, some staff must restrict activities and interactions with old people, which could lead to a devastating impact on residents' social connections [5,7]. Older people have different or interests or political thinking, so it is a challenge to match their needs through one particular method. The first research question (RQ1) is that what features could be suitable for a mapping procedure on a mutual algorithm to solve the manpower issues and alone living?

An effective method should be able to be customized with novel technologies to satisfy personal needs and preferences. Older people may have dynamic preferences even under the same features conditions, which may influence the chance of success when building a mutual algorithm. Therefore, the second research question is described as follows. RQ2: What kinds of mapping architectures and technologies can help us to build an effective mapping procedure based on the proposed mutual algorithm to coordinate human variability and privacy protection?

The motivation of the article is to clearly identify and solve the existing issues in long-term care to keep older people living safe and happy, and offer related organizations a solution to the shortage of manpower. The expected contributions include (1) solving existing issues on shortage of manpower on taking care of older people; (2) considering the fitness of the corporation for both sides for long-term care; (3) adjusting dynamically based on the human variety of characters; (4) recording the process and outcome of taking care of older people to be credited for the next arrangement; and (5) helping to measure the degree of the physical situation based on the records. An effective mutual algorithm should not only consider features related to personal characteristics and human variability, but also be able to record and improve collaboration or transaction processes through a highly trusted and rigid platform. The primary target of this study is to identify more accurate personal characteristics that can fit the mapping procedure. In addition, it aims to implement Artificial Intelligence (AI) based on a suitable mapping architecture to make the empirical process of the system both appropriate and reliable.

2. Architecture Theories

An ideal architecture of long-term care should consider whether or not it can bring older people a good service quality. Service quality of long-term care has been put in evaluating the long-term service from their perceptions [8]. Older people are interested in quality of the long-term care system including health care provided. Most of the studies showed that long-term care providers do not always pay attention on the quality of services provided. Service quality can be used as a strategic tool for building distinctive features. Literature shows that service quality can be divided into dimensions such as technical and process functional dimension [9]. Technical dimension on long-term care is defined as primarily on the basis of architecture design for maintaining good quality on the medical diagnoses and procedures services, as well as conformance to professional specification and standards such as centralized and the decentralized architecture of long-term cares [10]. Functional dimension can be defined to refer to the manner of long-term care service is delivered to quality of older people relationship with the caregivers.

2.1. The Centralized Architecture of Long-Term Care

The centralized architecture of long-term care is the process by which the activities of long-term care agents who can offer caregivers. The caregivers are like insurance agents who would be trained, have care permits, and would be assigned to a set of older people. However, this is not simply a problem of financial centralization or decentralization. The agent caregivers may seek to take care of nice people and avoid some older people who are at the high-risk levels of uncomfortable people. Centralization of access to the agents of long-term care through specialized data services could have security or privacy issues to lead to the protection failure of the personal data of older people [9,10].

Traditionally, the centralized architecture of long-term care could have the decision-making power to be managed directly with the agents of long-term care. Due to saving cost, centralization of long-term care aims at ensuring effective enforcement of controlling activities of caregiver's consistency in operation [9,10]. Therefore, the centralized architecture of long-term care, unlike many security agencies or entities in the human world, could have mutual problems because of unsuitable personality to let older people feel uncomfortable or lonely soul. In addition, privacy issues on personal data protection and insufficient manpower offered by agents of long-term care could be also serious problems through this the centralized architecture of long-term care.

2.2. The Decentralized Architecture of Long-Term Care

It is very important to consider service quality of caregivers based on the centralized architecture of long-term care. However, measuring service quality in long-term care is very difficult to evaluate. This is due to the fact that evaluation of understanding of real perceptions of older people and their satisfaction is quite complex [8]. Different agents may provide the same types of services but different quality of services. Decentralization of long-term care is the process of shifting decision making a way from centralized control and closer to older people themselves of the services. In many countries the government has opted to decentralize health system as means of improving responsiveness and performance of delivering of long-term care [10]. The decentralized architecture of long-term care has impacts on the performance of the systems based on some studies found [11,12]. In the decentralized architecture of long-term care, it still needs a way or create a model to handle the healthcare services because three main issues, including mental problems from unsuitable matches, privacy data of older people, and insufficient manpower, can be very important to contain the good service quality of caregivers.

Existing studies present a personal information management, which can offer specific features such as interests or contact lists related to the characteristics of older people, to manage communication through a centralized cloud system [13–16]. The basic idea behind the decentralized architecture of long-term care to replace or support human resource agencies or other specific local platforms as controlled centers is that good services can consider all human resources to adjust to or coordinate their needs [17]. Existing studies still try to offer cloud services to achieve sharing medical data with entities with minimal data privacy [18]. Although existing studies suggest using smart contracts to track the behavior of violations of data permissions, the current studies have some serious problems since it does not consider other impacts for older people such as risk levels. In addition, one of the common limitations of those approaches is that many older people long for a social network in order to have regular interaction with one another to manage spiritual loneliness, and they lack a platform for mutual algorithm and adjusted abilities based on a mapping process suitable for older people [19]. To the second research question, one of the major challenges is to face in this field is to explore a process innovation [20] in search of this answer. In order to solve the second research question and the problems mentioned above, this study proposes the use of the decentralized architecture of long-term care to store a mapping or transaction procedure based on AI methods, and the information would be secured and shared across all network candidates.

3. The Mutual Algorithm

When older people are engaging in their daily activities, they may defer or give up their current activities to take part in a mutual algorithm effort. Accordingly, a good mutual algorithm should consider if older people prefer to continue working on their main tasks and be given the opportunity to defer a mutual algorithm until they have completed their current activities. This also implies that a good mutual algorithm can allow older people to flow in and out freely, helping them to realize any rationalization and optimization from their participation in the structure. Older people are often highly active, unlike those in nursing care with chronic diseases, so it is necessary to consider their willingness to collaborate.

Clustering is one of the unsupervised learning methods in the field of machine learning, and it includes various algorithms that may differ significantly in the cluster analysis and efficiently identify factors across similar features [21,22]. This study uses the mapping mutual clustering (i.e., MMC) algorithm referred by the clustering method in the long-term care field. Based on the mutual features mapping mutual algorithm selection, this study assumes that each mapping round is repeated and there is an outcome (i.e., optimization) for each round. Therefore, the feedback of each collaboration should consider both the feedback and the probability of using the proposed mutual algorithm.

To formalize the mutual algorithm, this study formulates older people as a four-element vector, O_n (R_i, P_i, M_i, D_i), where n is the total older number of people in the mutual algorithm; $i = 1, 2, 3$; and terms O, R, P, M, D represent older people, risk level, physiology, medical record, and demography, respectively. Distances are normally used to measure the similarity or dissimilarity between two older people, so S (O_s, O_t) refers to the similarity between two older people, $s = (s1, s2, \ldots, si)$, and $t = (t1, t2, \ldots, ti)$. The similarity function of mapping process for each person is defined in Equation (1):

$$S(O_s, O_t) = \sqrt[q]{(O_{s1} - O_{t1})^q + (O_{s2} - O_{t2})^q + \ldots + (O_{si} - O_{ti})^q} \qquad (1)$$

According to Equation (1), this study continues to compute the minimum similarity distance of older people in the same group into K nonempty subsets in Equation (2):

$$K_{S\,(O_s,\,O_t)} = \min(\sum_{l=1}^{n} S_l) \qquad (2)$$

According to Equation (2), the mutual algorithm continues to compute seed older people as the centroids of the current clusters: $M_1, M_2, \ldots, M_k$, and then the mutual algorithm uses S (O_s, O_t) to subtract M_k to obtain a new S (O_s, O_t) for Equation (3) and new K groups in Equation (4):

$$S_{new}\,(O_s,\,O_t) = S\,(O_s,\,O_t) - M_k\,(K_{S\,(O_s,\,O_t)}) \qquad (3)$$

$$K_{S_{new}\,(O_s,\,O_t)} = \min(\sum_{l=1}^{n} S_{new\,l}) \qquad (4)$$

To test MMC, the process of implementation is used to identify initialization of parameters, setting groups, computing similarity, and building final mutual algorithm. The basic idea of the mutual algorithm is that the mapping mutual clustering (MMC) is implemented as an algorithm called the mutual algorithm (Algorithm 1), which can identify some features of older people such as risk level, and group them based on these features. The mutual algorithm is a finite sequence of well-defined, computer-implementable instructions for the mutual algorithm in order to perform a computation upon evaluation. The detailed description of the mutual algorithm is clear as follows, and it is possible to evaluate and verify its feasibility and correctness by building the measurable architecture described in the next subsection to be implemented through the evaluation plan. In the mutual algorithm, there are several steps that need to be implemented, (1) setting initialization of parameters such as risk level, medical record, etc. of older people; (2) giving an original group based on the first glance; (3) resetting their groups based the later features by using clustering to dynamically adjust for human variety characters; (4) building new corporation relationships and making arrangements based on the novel matching way on step three.

Algorithm 1. Implementation of the Mapping Mutual Clustering (MMC) Algorithm

1. Require: Initialization of parameters:
getRiskLevel, getPhysiology, getMedicalRecord, getDemography, getOlderPeopleID
2. Set up groups:
groupA (getOlderPeopleID) ← groupA (getRiskLevel, getPhysiology, getMedicalRecord, getDemography)
groupB (getOlderPeopleID) ← groupB (getRiskLevel, getPhysiology, getMedicalRecord, getDemography)
groupC (getOlderPeopleID) ← groupC (getRiskLevel, getPhysiology, getMedicalRecord, getDemography)
3. Compute similarity:
for groupA ()
  groupA (getOlderPeopleID) ← retrieve (minimum distance)
end for groupA ()
for groupB ()
  groupB (getOlderPeopleID) ← retrieve (minimum distance)
end for groupB ()
for groupC ()
  groupC (getOlderPeopleID) ← retrieve (minimum distance)
end for groupC ()
4. Build collaboration:
if groupA (getOlderPeopleID) > groupB (getOlderPeopleID) > groupC (getOlderPeopleID) then
    groupA (getOlderPeopleID) ← assign (groupC (getOlderPeopleID))
else if groupA (getOlderPeopleID) > groupC (getOlderPeopleID) > groupB (getOlderPeopleID) then
groupA (getOlderPeopleID) ← assign (groupB (getOlderPeopleID))
else if groupB (getOlderPeopleID) > groupA (getOlderPeopleID) > groupC (getOlderPeopleID) then
    groupB (getOlderPeopleID) ← assign (groupC (getOlderPeopleID))
else if groupB (getOlderPeopleID) > groupC (getOlderPeopleID) > groupA (getOlderPeopleID) then
    groupB (getOlderPeopleID) ← assign (groupA (getOlderPeopleID))
else if groupC (getOlderPeopleID) > groupA (getOlderPeopleID) > groupB (getOlderPeopleID) then
    groupC (getOlderPeopleID) ← assign (groupB (getOlderPeopleID))
else
    groupC (getOlderPeopleID) ← assign (groupA (getOlderPeopleID))
end if

According to the proposed mapping mutual clustering method and its implementation with the mutual algorithm as a description of the implementation of the mapping mutual clustering algorithm above, in order to build a long-term and comprehensive guideline for further system applications, it is necessary to build a framework called the decentralized self-service framework as Figure 1 depicted. The basic idea of the decentralized self-service framework is that the features are identified clearly with four factors including rick level, physiology, medical records, and demography, the steps are illustrated obviously from grouping to suitability, and the service is grouped into a kind of self-service, which can open to social networks. Based on extant approaches and their limitations, the proposed mutual algorithm not only integrates different data from diverse features but also considers utilizing a classification algorithm in Artificial Intelligence to dynamically increase accuracy. Therefore, adding a self-service mechanism is an important step before building the proposed the decentralized architecture of long-term care. The self-service framework is a grouping based on their similar backgrounds, finding relations of individual interaction; and learning by dynamic adjustment, and running suitably and successfully through mutual understanding.

The proposed architecture (LCDA) applies Blockchain technology to demonstrate trusted and auditable computing and the decentralized networks of all older people accompanied by a public collaborative ledger (Figure 2). LCDA can solve the issues of cost and time consumption related to data acquisition and inappropriate distribution relations between older people. In addition, this architecture can solve the existing issues of care agencies, which now are under third-party authorization. The proposed architecture also can save the costs of transmission and integration through quick and direct data exchanges between older people. Through this LCDA, the proposed mutual algorithm could ensure the non-destructibility of data, which can make the MMC be recorded of older people in a more secure way. The LCDA algorithm (Algorithm 2) demonstrates initialization of parameters from older people; setting up functions such as hash, encryption, and signature to ensure data of older people more secure; computing proof-of-work to let the system operate effectively; and adding blocks to ledgers to let the systems adjust dynamically.

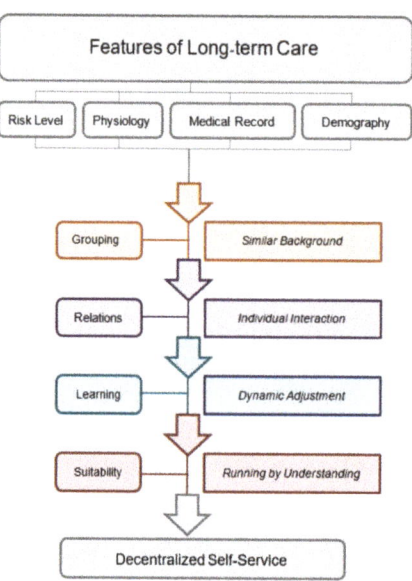

Figure 1. The Decentralized Self-Service Framework. In an existing centralized system, to make transparency more effective, this local server system must play a role in making fair and accurate reports available to the public [23,24]. The proposed decentralized architecture of long-term care represents that older people's information and availability are important features for the mutual algorithm [25]. Through the decentralized architecture of long-term care (called long-term care decentralized architecture (i.e., LCDA)), this not only reduces the cost compared to centralized systems, but also eliminates the chances of information loss due to a single point of failure, since ledger copies are synchronized across all older people.

Algorithm 2. Implementation of the Long-term Care Decentralized Architecture (LCDA) Algorithm

---

1. **Require: Initialization of parameters:**
  getOlderPeopleID, getOlderPeopleRecords
2. **Set up functions:**
  hash (getOlderPeopleID, getOlderPeopleRecords)
  encryption (getOlderPeopleID, getOlderPeopleRecords)
  signature (getOlderPeopleID, getOlderPeopleRecords)
3. **Compute proof-of-work:**
  for pow (time)
  constructing blocks ← hashcash (getOlderPeopleID) == true
  end for
4. **Add blocks to ledgers:**
  if constructing blocks == true then
  confidential transactions ← hash () + encryption () + signature ()
    upchain to the decentralized platform
    end if
  decryption (getOlderPeopleID, getOlderPeopleRecords)

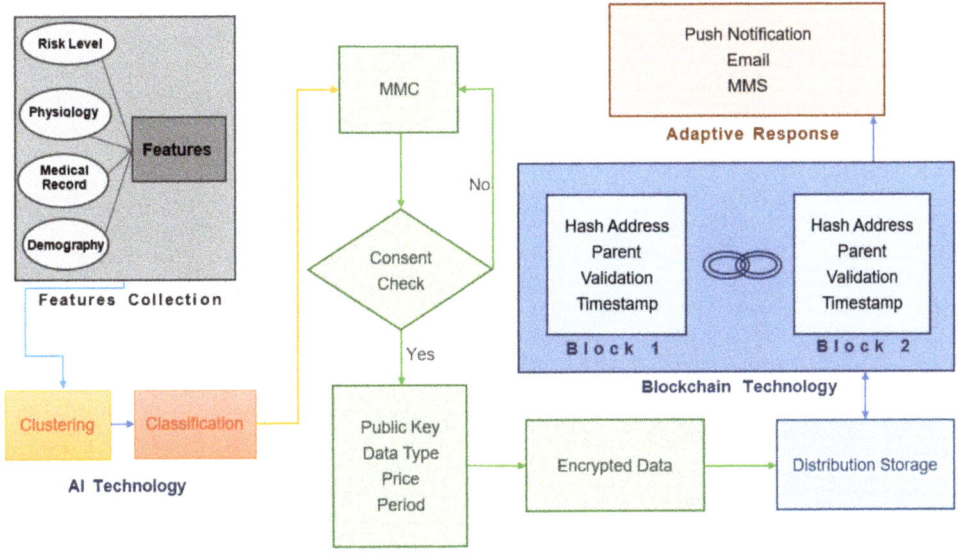

Figure 2. Long-term Care Decentralized Architecture (LCDA).

The mapping or transaction procedure is a type of distributed ledger, which can view transactions anytime to make LCDA immutable and irreversible.

4. Research Model

This study proposes methods including the mapping mutual clustering (MMC) algorithm and the long-term care decentralized architecture (LCDA) algorithm for creating an innovative manner to solve problems as research questions described. The user perceptions can include user satisfaction, ease of use, usefulness, and user intention, which are all popular for evaluating systems [26,27]. To evaluate the system proposed as RQ1 mentioned, this first hypothesis considers medical records, risk level, physiology, and demography to improve the users' perceived usefulness, ease of use, satisfaction, and intention to use the long-term care system.

The research model (Figure 3) mainly focuses on the support vector machines (SVMs), which is widely-used algorithm [28] for risk minimization [29,30]. Other algorithms such as the random forest is suitable for classification trees to put the input vector down each tree in the forest [30].

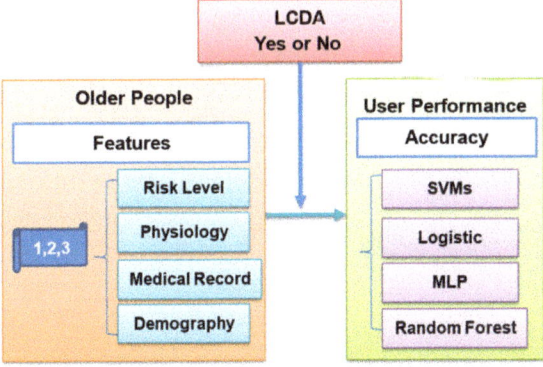

Figure 3. Research Model.

This research also uses LCDA to solve the issues of human variability. According to the second research question (RQ2), the second hypothesis examines whether or not the accuracy of the LCDA is higher than the mutual algorithm without the proposed method. The detailed description of the MMC and LCDA algorithm is very clear in the previous two sections, and it is possible to evaluate and verify its feasibility and correctness by building the measurable research model and implementing it through the evaluation plan.

5. Experiment Design

Twelve participants were randomly recruited from various locations (e.g., nursing home, hospital, park) to fill out a questionnaire in order to collect features data (https://drive.google.com/file/d/1rvx-T9krnsZ-ErRgl-wESieP2qFnBfos/view?usp=sharing, accessed on 1 January 2022) of LCDA. To help participants understand LCDA, the prototype system (Figure 4) has been developed with mobile application software to assist them in completing the questionnaire successfully.

Participants were over 65 years old. All participants were informed that any potentially identifying information learned and collected from this study would remain confidential and disclosed only upon receipt of permission from the participant. There are three levels for each factor. For the risk level factor, if older people consider that they do not require assistance from others most of the time, this is Level 1. If they estimate a nearly fifty-fifty chance that they need care from others, it is Level 2. The remaining risk level is Level 3. Older people can refer to their own Barthel index, as assessed by the government, to complete this part. Other features such as physiology, medical record, and demography are also classified according to three levels as shown in Table 1. The survey questionnaire about whether or not the proposed system can improve users' (a) perceived usefulness, (b) ease of use, (c) satisfaction, and (d) intention to use for long-term care. A five-point Likert scale [31] was used with 1 indicating "strongly disagree,", 3 indicating "neutral," and 5 indicating "strongly agree".

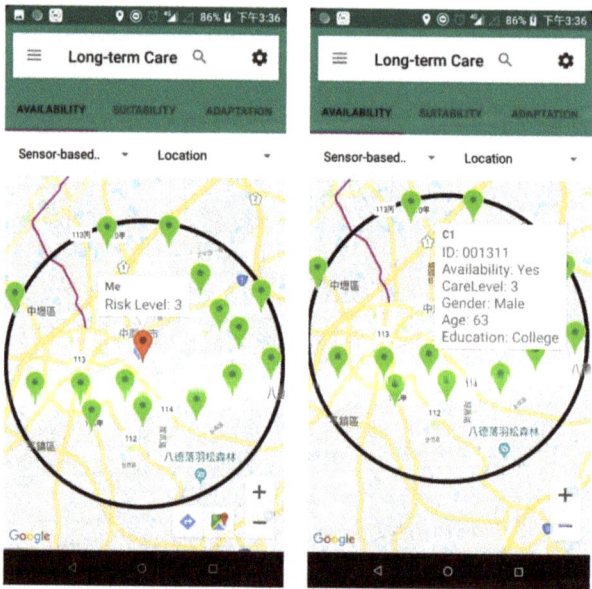

Figure 4. The Prototype System of Long-term Care.

The system architecture (Figure 5) uses Android Studio software for designing Java programming and mobile application services (APPs).

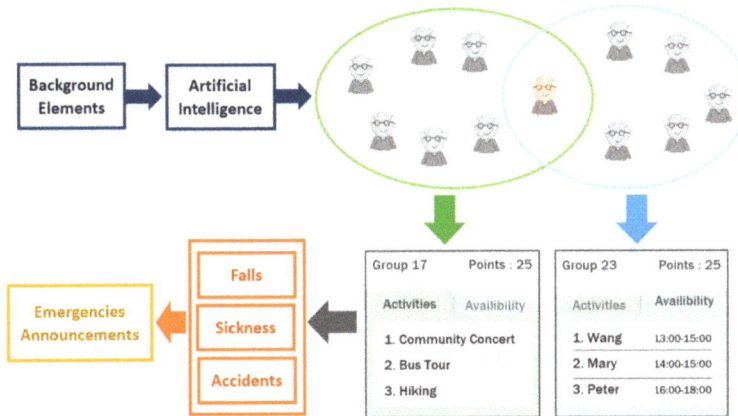

Figure 5. The System Architecture of the Prototype System.

Table 1. Levels of Features of LCDA.

Level	Risk Level	Physiology	Medical Record	Demography
1	Independence	Stand + Walk	No disease	Well-educated
2	Independence + Help	Stand + Walk + Help	Minor disease	Basic education
3	Help	Help	Major disease	No education

6. Results

For the first hypothesis, Cronbach's alpha for user perception was 0.88, which revealed the consistency is reliable. A one-sample t-test is used for evaluating whether or not the average of user perception is equal to 3 (neutral) based on the middle point of Likert scale [32]. The perceived usefulness mean difference is 1.33 ($p < 0.01$), perceived ease of use is 1.29 ($p < 0.01$), user satisfaction is 0.96 ($p < 0.01$), and user intention mean difference is 1.17 ($p < 0.01$) are all significant. Therefore, the first hypothesis is supported. The data of all participants were collected from the questionnaire based on the proposed features shown in Table 2.

Table 2. Dataset of Participant Features.

Person	Risk Level	Physiology	Medical Record	Demography
P1	2	1	1	2
P2	2	2	2	2
P3	1	1	1	1
P4	3	2	1	2
P5	2	3	2	1
P6	2	2	1	3
P7	1	3	1	3
P8	3	1	2	1
P9	2	3	1	3
P10	1	2	2	2
P11	1	2	3	1
P12	3	3	3	3

According to the MMC steps (1–3), including initial partition for older people, choosing seeds as temporary center members, and assigning older people to new groups based on the similarity computations, the dataset is represented in Tables 3–5, respectively.

Table 3. Similarity of Initial Partition for Older People.

	P1	P5	P9
P1	0	2.449489743	2.236067977
P2	1.414213562	1.414213562	1.732050808
P3	1.414213562	2.449489743	3
P4	1.414213562	2	1.732050808
P5	2.449489743	0	2.236067977
P6	1.414213562	2.449489743	1
P7	2.449489743	2.449489743	1
P8	1.732050808	2.236067977	3.16227766
P9	2.236067977	2.236067977	0
P10	1.732050808	1.732050808	2
P11	2.645751311	1.732050808	3.16227766
P12	3.16227766	2.449489743	2.236067977

Table 4. Temporary Groups Based on the Similarity.

N1	P1	P2	P3	P4	P8	P10
N2	P5	P11				
N3	P6	P7	P9	P12		

Table 5. Center Means of Temporary Groups.

	Risk Level	Physiology	Medical Record	Demography
C1	2	1.5	1.5	2
C2	1.5	2.5	2.5	1
C3	2	3	1	3

According to the center means of temporary groups, this study continues to compute the minimum similarity distance of older people for the temporary and final groups as shown in Tables 6 and 7, respectively.

Table 6. Similarity of Temporary Groups for Older People.

	C1	C2	C3
P1	0.707106781	2.397915762	2.236067977
P2	0.707106781	1.322875656	1.732050808
P3	1.58113883	2.179449472	3
P4	1.224744871	2.397915762	1.732050808
P5	1.870828693	0.866025404	2.236067977
P6	1.224744871	2.598076211	1
P7	2.121320344	2.598076211	1
P8	1.58113883	2.179449472	3.16227766
P9	1.870828693	2.598076211	0
P10	1.224744871	1.322875656	2
P11	2.121320344	0.866025404	3.16227766
P12	2.549509757	2.598076211	2.236067977

Table 7. Final Groups Based on MMC.

F1	P1	P2	P3	P4	P8	P10
F2	P5	P11				
F3	P6	P7	P9	P12		

The dataset of features of older people includes RL1, Phy1, MR1, Dem1, RL2, Phy2, MR2, and Dem2 to represent the risk level, physiology, medical record, and demography, respectively (Table 8). The LCDA dataset shows a total of 66 observations calculated in Equation (5):

$$\sum_{i=1, j=1, i \neq j}^{12} Combination\ (i,j) = C_2^{12} = \frac{12!}{2! * 10!} = 66 \qquad (5)$$

Table 8. LCDA Dataset of Older People.

RL1	Phy1	MR1	Dem1	RL2	Phy2	MR2	Dem2	LCDA
2	2	1	3	1	3	1	3	Y
2	1	1	2	1	2	3	1	N
2	2	1	3	3	3	3	3	Y
2	1	1	2	2	3	1	3	N
1	3	1	3	3	3	3	3	Y
2	3	1	3	3	3	3	3	Y
2	1	1	2	2	3	2	1	N
~	~	~	~	~	~	~	~	~
2	1	1	2	2	2	1	3	N
2	3	1	3	3	3	3	3	Y
2	1	1	2	2	3	1	3	N
2	2	2	2	2	3	2	1	N

The accuracies are 86.36%, 96.97%, 98.48%, and 98.48% using SVMs, logistic, and MLP, random forest, respectively. The MLP and random forests achieve the highest level of accuracy (Figure 6).

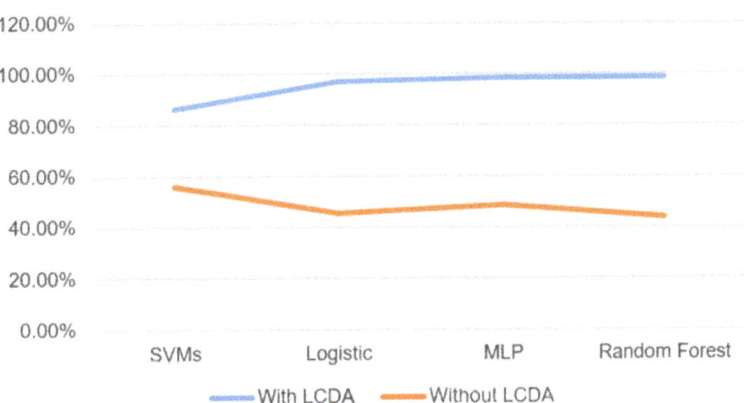

Figure 6. Accuracy of Classification Algorithms.

The collaboration is built randomly 66 times, and the highest accuracy is 56.06% from SVMs. The mean difference is -30.3 ($p < 0.01$), which is significant. Therefore, the second hypothesis is also supported.

7. Discussion

Based on the literature review, currently, the design of long-term care intends to use centralized architecture, which means agencies assign caretakers to older people based on their manpower policies without taking the appropriate characteristics of older people into consideration. The study proposed methods including MMC and LCDA to overcome some important issues based on the existing architecture that could lead to shortages of manpower and inappropriate cooperation between caretakers and older people. After being systematically evaluated in the experiment, the hypotheses are all supported, those issues can be confirmed to be solved by using the proposed mapping mutual clustering method and long-term care decentralized architecture. Older people sense the suitable caretakers around them, cognitively group caretakers by some characteristics generated from MMC, form long-term corporation relationships with LCDA, and generate records in order to adjust groups dynamically.

With the proposed methods, older people can involve and generate a corporate process when realistic circumstances are acted out in the long-term care systems in order to better understand the outcome of caretakers no matter they are coming from. Because individual caretakers may behave differently attitudes or performance even under the same situation, attempting to define the qualified ability of caretakers and associated system reactions in a static way that is desired by all older people is impossible and can result in risks and difficulty for caretakers. Therefore, a long-term care system should provide a dynamic interaction for all participants so that they can map mutual rules at any time. The decentralized architecture emphasizes the importance of understanding older people in their mapping mutual process and involves characteristics such as risk level while going out for a walk in a dangerous environment.

8. Conclusions

The study makes many significant contributions to proposing novel methods. First, existing mutual algorithms for long-term care mainly focus on benefits with centralized care agencies to match healthcare workers and older people. However, the benefits of care agencies and cannot solve the issue of manpower. To address the first research question, this study proposes a novel method, called the mapping mutual clustering algorithm, considering all possible features across all older people. Second, the proposed long-term care decentralized architecture algorithm applies Artificial Intelligence and Blockchain to solve the issues of dynamically adjusting, coordinating human variability, and the privacy protection, which can address the second research question. Third, this study applies an empirical process to long-term care.

There are a few limitations and future works to this study. First, this study evaluated the proposed decentralized architecture of long-term care through a features-based questionnaire, which could not immediately reflect current long-term care operational mechanisms in reality. Therefore, it is better to perform an experiment with a larger sample based on the proposed methods in future studies. In the future, enlarging the dataset by building the decentralized system will overcome any limitation on the accuracy of the classification. Second, due to considering privacy issues, the relevant features categorized on the risk levels 1, 2, and 3 do not correspond to the Barthel index, as measured by official investigation reports. To guide practical insights to the long-term care system, the sub-item categories should be clearly identified to solve the issue of disclosing information.

Funding: This research received no external funding.

Institutional Review Board Statement: This article does not contain any studies on human risk performed by any of the authors.

Informed Consent Statement: This article can exclude the informed consent statement due to no human risk performed by any of the authors.

Data Availability Statement: The data that support the findings of this study are available in https://drive.google.com/file/d/1rvx-19krnsZ-ErRgl-wESieP2qFnBfos/view?usp=sharing (accessed on 1 January 2022).

Acknowledgments: I would like to thank my research assistant Yu-Tzu Lu for her help in collecting the long-term care data.

Conflicts of Interest: Author Hsien-Ming Chou declares that he has no conflict of interest.

References

1. Wang, H.-H.; Tsay, S.-F. Elderly and long-term care trends and policy in Taiwan: Challenges and opportunities of health care professionals. *Kaohsiung J. Med. Sci.* **2012**, *28*, 465–469. [CrossRef] [PubMed]
2. Chou, H.M. A Collaborative Framework with Artificial Intelligence for Long-term Care. *IEEE Access* **2020**, *8*, 43657–43664. [CrossRef]
3. Zhao, H.; Xiong, W.H.; Zhao, X.; Wang, L.M.; Chen, J.X. Development and evaluation of a traditional Chinese medicine syndrome questionnaire for measuring sub-optimal health status in China. *J. Tradit. Chin. Med.* **2012**, *32*, 129–136. [CrossRef]
4. Li, G.; Yan, S.; Hu, X.; Jin, B.; Wang, J.; Wu, J.; Yin, D.; Xie, Q. Subhealth: Definition, criteria for diagnosis and potential prevalence in the central region of China. *BMC Public Health* **2013**, *4*, 446. [CrossRef] [PubMed]
5. Heras, E.; Garibaldi, P.; Boix, M.; Valero, O.; Castillo, J.; Curbelo, Y.; Gonzalez, E.; Mendoza, O.; Anglada, M.; Miralles, J.C.; et al. COVID-19 mortality risk factors in older people in a long-term care center. *Eur. Geriatr. Med.* **2021**, *12*, 601–607. [CrossRef]
6. Bethell, J.; Aelick, K.; Babineau, J.; Bretzlaff, M.; Edwards, C.; Gibson, J.-L.; Colborne, D.H.; Iaboni, A.; Lender, D.; Schon, D.; et al. Social connection in long-term care homes: A scoping review of published research on the mental health impacts and potential strategies during COVID-19. *JAMDA* **2021**, *22*, 228–237. [CrossRef] [PubMed]
7. Chu, C.H.; Donato-Woodger, S.; Dainton, C.J. Competing crises: COVID-19 countermeasures and social isolation among older adults in long-term care. *J. Adv. Nurs.* **2020**, *76*, 2456–2459. [CrossRef] [PubMed]
8. Padma, P.; Rajendran, C.; Sai, L.P. A conceptual framework of service quality in healthcare. *Benchmarking Int. J.* **2009**, *16*, 157–191. [CrossRef]
9. Kitapci, O.; Akdogan, C.; Dortyol, I.T. The impact of SQ dimensions on patient satisfaction, repurchase intentions and word-of-mouth communication in the public healthcare industry. *Procedia Soc. Behav. Sci.* **2014**, *148*, 161–169. [CrossRef]
10. Mishra, V.; Samuel, C.; Sharma, S.K. Decision of decentralization in a healthcare service—A case of diabetes management. *Int. J. Healthc. Manag.* **2018**, *12*, 308–313. [CrossRef]
11. Tediosi, F.; Gabriele, S.; Longo, F. Governing decentralization in health care under tough budget constraint: What can we learn from the Italian experience? *Health Policy* **2009**, *90*, 303–312. [CrossRef] [PubMed]
12. Collins, C.; Green, A. Decentralization and primary health care: Some negative implications in developing countries. *Int. J. Health Serv.* **1994**, *24*, 459–475. [CrossRef]
13. Parker, S.G.; Peet, S.M.; McPherson, A.; Cannaby, A.M.; Abrams, K.R.; Baker, R.; Wilson, A.; Lindesay, J.; Parker, G.; Jones, D.R. A systematic review of discharge arrangements for older people. *Health Technol. Assess.* **2002**, *6*, 1–183. [CrossRef]
14. Bragstad, L.K.; Kirkevold, M.; Hofoss, D.; Foss, C. Factors predicting a successful post-discharge outcome for individuals aged 80 years and over. *Int. J. Integr. Care* **2012**, *12*, e147. [CrossRef]
15. Zhang, L.; Ahn, G.; Chu, B. A role-based delegation framework for healthcare information systems. In Proceedings of the ACM Symposium on Access Control Models and Technologies (SACMAT 2002), Monterey, CA, USA, 3–4 June 2002; pp. 125–134.
16. Aslam, K.F.; Ali, A.; Abbas, H.; Haldar, N.H. A cloud-based healthcare framework for security and patients' data privacy using wireless body area networks. *Procedia Comput. Sci.* **2014**, *34*, 511–517.
17. Grozev, N.; Buyya, R. Inter-Cloud architectures and application brokering: Taxonomy and survey. *Softw. Pract. Exp.* **2014**, *44*, 369–390. [CrossRef]
18. Xia, Q.; Sifah, E.B.; Asamoah, K.O.; Gao, J.; Du, X.; Guizani, M. MeDShare: Trust-less medical data sharing among cloud service providers via blockchain. *IEEE Access* **2017**, *5*, 14757–14767. [CrossRef]
19. Weber, G.M.; Mandl, K.D.; Kohane, I.S. Finding the missing link for big biomedical data. *J. Am. Med. Assoc.* **2014**, *311*, 2479–2480. [CrossRef] [PubMed]
20. Omachonu, V.K.; Einspruch, N.G. Innovation in healthcare delivery systems: A conceptual framework. *Public Sect. Innov. J.* **2010**, *15*, 1–20.
21. Suganthi, R.; Kamalakannan, P. Analyzing stock market data using clustering algorithm. *Int. J. Future Comput. Commun.* **2015**, *4*, 108–111. [CrossRef]
22. Lughofer, E. Hybrid active learning for reducing the annotation effort of operators in classification systems. *Pattern Recognit.* **2012**, *45*, 884–896. [CrossRef]
23. Xia, Q.; Sifah, E.B.; Smah, A.; Amofa, S.; Zhang, X. BBDS: Blockchain-based data sharing for electronic medical records in cloud environments. *Information* **2017**, *8*, 44. [CrossRef]
24. Casino, F.; Dasaklis, T.K.; Patsakis, C. A systematic literature review of blockchain-based applications: Current status, classification and open issues. *Telemat. Inform.* **2019**, *36*, 55–81. [CrossRef]
25. Puthal, D.; Malik, N.; Mohanty, S.P.; Kougianos, E.; Yang, C. The blockchain as a decentralized security framework future directions. *IEEE Consum. Electron. Mag.* **2018**, *7*, 18–21. [CrossRef]
26. Radner, R.; Rothschild, M. On the allocation of effort. *J. Econ. Theory* **1975**, *10*, 358–376. [CrossRef]
27. Davis, F.D. Perceived usefulness, perceived ease of use, and user acceptance of information technology. *MIS Q.* **1989**, *13*, 319–340. [CrossRef]
28. Krause, A.; Smailagic, A.; Siewiorek, D.P. Context-aware mobile computing: Learning context-dependent personal preferences from a wearable sensor array. *IEEE Trans. Mob. Comput.* **2006**, *5*, 113–127. [CrossRef]
29. Frénay, B.; Verleysen, M. Using SVMs with randomised feature spaces: An extreme learning approach. Proceedings of Computational Intelligence and Machine Learning, Bruges, Belgium, 28–30 April 2010.

30. Kremic, E.; Subasi, A. Performance of random forest and SVM in face recognition. *Int. Arab J. Inf. Technol.* **2016**, *13*, 287–293.
31. Lewis, J.R. IBM computer usability satisfaction questionnaires: Psychometric evaluation and instructions for use. *Int. J. Hum. Comput. Interact.* **1995**, *7*, 57–78. [CrossRef]
32. Chen, D.N.; Hu, P.J.H.; Kuo, Y.R.; Liang, T.P. A Web-based personalized recommendation system for mobile phone selection: Design, implementation, and evaluation. *Expert Syst. Appl.* **2010**, *37*, 8201–8210. [CrossRef]

Article

Proxy Re-Encryption Scheme for Decentralized Storage Networks

Jia Kan [1,2,†], Jie Zhang [1,†], Dawei Liu [3] and Xin Huang [2,*]

1. Department of Communications and Networking, Xi'an Jiaotong-Liverpool University, Suzhou 215123, China; jia.kan19@student.xjtlu.edu.cn (J.K.); jie.zhang01@xjtlu.edu.cn (J.Z.)
2. College of Data Science, Taiyuan University of Technology, Taiyuan 030024, China
3. Cyber Technology Institute, De Montfort University, Leicester LE1 9BH, UK; dawei.liu@dmu.ac.uk
* Correspondence: huangxin@tyut.edu.cn
† These authors contributed equally to this work.

Abstract: Storage is a promising application for permission-less blockchains. Before blockchain, cloud storage was hosted by a trusted service provider. The centralized system controls the permission of the data access. In web3, users own their data. Data must be encrypted in a permission-less decentralized storage network, and the permission control should be pure cryptographic. Proxy re-encryption (PRE) is ideal for cryptographic access control, which allows a proxy to transfer Alice's ciphertext to Bob with Alice's authorization. The encrypted data are stored in several copies for redundancy in a permission-less decentralized storage network. The redundancy suffers from the outsourcing attack. The malicious resource provider may fetch the content from others and respond to the verifiers. This harms data integrity security. Thus, proof-of-replication (PoRep) must be applied to convince the user that the storage provider is using dedicated storage. PoRep is an expensive operation that encodes the original content into a replication. Existing PRE schemes cannot satisfy PoRep, as the cryptographic permission granting generates an extra ciphertext. A new ciphertext would result in several expensive replication operations. We searched most of the PRE schemes for the combination of the cryptographic methods to avoid transforming the ciphertext. Therefore, we propose a new PRE scheme. The proposed scheme does not require the proxy to transfer the ciphertext into a new one. It reduces the computation and operation time when allowing a new user to access a file. Furthermore, the PRE scheme is CCA (chosen-ciphertext attack) security and only needs one key pair.

Keywords: proxy re-encryption; blockchain; storage; proof-of-replication

1. Introduction

Blockchain technology has been actively developing in recent years. A decentralized storage network [1] based on the blockchain is a promising application direction. The decentralized storage network would redefine data ownership, privacy, and accessibility. Taking the example of the traffic surveillance cameras, the data may be stored on a decentralized storage network. Therefore, the public can verify that the data exist, but only authorized parties can access it. Multiple institutions (such as insurance companies) to access data require an encryption scheme with access control. Traditional symmetric or asymmetric cryptography cannot meet this requirement, as these schemes require specifying who can decrypt before encrypting. The proxy re-encryption (PRE) is a suitable scheme for data sharing.

PRE allows a user to grant access permission in a cryptographic method. Alice would allow Bob to visit her data under Alice's authorization. However, the ciphertext must be transferred to the new one (Figure 1). In a decentralized storage network, data integration suffers from the challenge of the outsourcing attack. Blockchain consists of many semi-trusted resource providers. When asked for proof, the malicious provider would download the data content from other honest providers on the fly. Proof-of-replication (PoRep) brings the concept against the outsourcing attack. The idea is to encode the user data with a unique key, e.g., the provider's public key. Meanwhile, the encoding algorithm should be expensive, and decoding is cheap, so the resource provider would not drop the replicated data, as regenerating the replication would cost more. Since everyone tends to reduce the cost, the data would lose redundancy without PoRep. PoRep is the mandatory algorithm to convenience the verifiers that the dedicating storage resource is spending.

Existing PRE is not ideal for a decentralized storage network because the extra ciphertext would trigger an expensive replicating operation (Figure 2). Combined with PoRep, the cost of PRE sharing is too high.

We propose a CCA (chosen ciphertext attack)-secure and collusion-resilience (collusion safe) proxy re-encryption scheme for the decentralized storage network (Figure 3).

1. No new ciphertext is generated for the permission grant in a decentralized storage network. It brings down the cost for proof-of-replication in a permission-less decentralized storage network.
2. The collusion-resilience scheme in group algebra requires only one key pair.

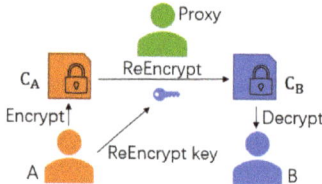

Figure 1. Traditional PRE requires proxy computation to re-encrypt.

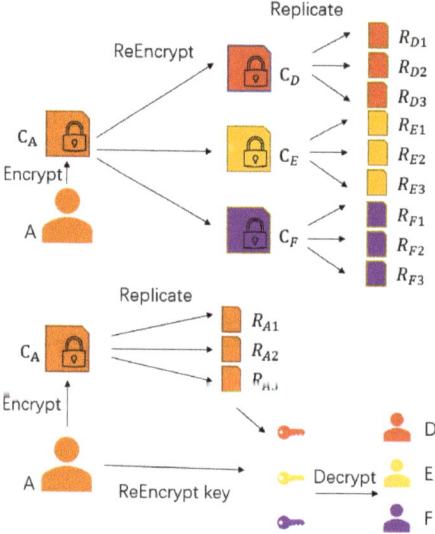

Figure 2. Comparison of the replication in decentralized storage network with or without transferred ciphertext.

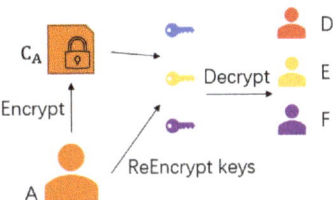

Figure 3. Our PRE scheme use C_A and ReEncrypt key to decrypt.

The rest of the paper is organized as follows. In Section 2, we talk about the detail of decentralized storage networks and proxy re-encryption. In Section 3, we dive into the knowledge, terms, and formula used in this work. The proposed scheme and security analysis are presented in Section 4. In Section 5 we give a practical implementation and show the experiment result. The various extended questions are talked about in the evaluation, Section 6. Finally, Sections 7 and 8 provide the conclusion and future work.

2. Related Work

This section will dive deep into the background of the decentralized storage network, blockchain, and its relationship with proxy re-encryption.

2.1. Decentralized Storage Network

The cloud service is provided by a trusted third party. The data permission is controlled with a centralized mechanism. With the blockchain innovation, the recent study shows that the decentralized storage network is viable [1–4]. In the decentralized storage network, the user is not required to trust any providers, just the cryptography. It brings enormous confidence to the data owner.

The decentralized storage network is ideally built upon a permission-less blockchain. Blockchain miners provide the storage resource. The content that a user uploads to the blockchain is kept by miners. The blockchain makes the storage network permission-less. The miners can freely join or quit.

In the decentralized storage network, permission control must be cryptographic since the storage providers are semi-trusted. The existing public-key crypto is required to specify the target user to decrypt before encryption. Beyond this, PRE allows users to add the target users by re-encrypt the existing ciphertext into a new one. It is identical to permission granting at the application level. Thus, PRE schemes are helpful for blockchain storage.

However, a decentralized storage network must periodically check content integrity. The malicious miner may cheat by fetching content from other honest miners and responding to the checking. The cheater is committing to keep the content but never spending the storage resource. A decentralized storage network must be resilient to the outsourcing attack. Proof-of-replication requires the miners to encode the user content into the replication with each miner's unique identity. It is intended to make the encoding more expensive. The miner is willing to save the replication on disk, as it is impossible to fetch the content from other miners and finish the encoding in the limited time.

2.2. Proxy Re-Encryption and Proof-of-Replication

In 1998, Blaze, Bleumer, and Strauss [5] proposed the first proxy re-encryption scheme based on a cyclic group [6]. In 2010, Weng et al. [7] proposed a CCA and collusion-resilience PRE scheme. After 2010 [8,9], most PRE schemes were based on bilinear pairing [10–12] or lattice algebra structure [13]. The data uploaded must be encrypted in the decentralized storage network. However, most the PRE schemes are generating the new ciphertext during the re-encryption. A ciphertext would be replicated with each miners' unique identity. Any modification of the ciphertext would lead to more expensive PoRep operations. A PRE scheme is ideal not to generate new ciphertext during the frequent permission sharing actions under the decentralize storage network scenario. Thus, we propose the new PRE scheme.

While the new PRE schemes are diving into more complex algebra structure, the use scenarios of PRE are still limited. As business companies back the cloud service, the cloud and mobile do not fully utilize PRE schemes. The encryption will prevent data analysis and take extra cost of storage and computation. Owing to the blockchain, we foresee that blockchain-based decentralized applications will heavily rely on cryptographic schemes. Web3 allows the user to own their data. The decentralized storage network requires a pure cryptographic access control feature. PRE is ideal, but PoRep is mandatory.

The first blockchain, Bitcoin, proposed the proof-of-work (PoW) as the consensus algorithm [14] after PoW was used earlier for anti-spam purpose [15]. Computation was used as the resource for consensus, such as voting. Later, the storage space as a resource was studied, which can be classified into two categories. The proof-of-space intends to replace proof-of-work as the consensus algorithm. This replacement can bring down the cost of electricity by PoW, but junk data needs to be filled in the hard disk so far. Conversely, the proof-of-storage algorithm focuses on storing useful data. However, this algorithm cannot agree on a consensus. It only shows the proof of the data stored. Proof-of-replication is an extension of proof-of-storage, which convinces the owner that the unique storage resource keeps the data. In the permission-less blockchain, the PoRep is the key algorithm. It is nice to design schemes working with PoRep for the storage features. Filecoin uses SDR as the PoRep encoding and proves with the zero-knowledge-based algorithm [2,3]. Filecoin lets users decide how to encrypt their data. Therefore, there is no cryptographic access control for decentralized storage networks yet. The improved PRE scheme is worth studying.

In 1998, Blaze, Bleumer, and Strauss [5] proposed the first proxy re-encryption scheme. The ciphertext can be re-encrypted into another by the proxy authorized by the owner. Although the first PRE scheme is not collusion-resilient, it shows the possibility to change the key or password of the ciphertext without decryption. In 2003, Ivan and Dodis [16] proposed the group-based proxy cryptography scheme. In their unidirectional scheme, the secret key is first divided into two parts. This is the main technique that is used for collusion safety by many schemes. This illuminates our idea. In 2009, Shao et al. [17] proposed a CCA-secure scheme without pairing. Their scheme uses double trapdoors with the big prime multiplication as the secret key. One year later, Weng et al. [7] proposed a CCA-secure scheme WDLC10 without pairing. Two key pairs are used to avoid collusion for the secret key in their scheme, which is similar to Ivan and Dodis [16]. In the following years, most CCA-secure schemes were based on bilinear pairing or lattice. The PRE schemes such as AFGH06 [18] and GA07 [19] are based on bilinear pairing. XT10 [20] and ABPW13 [21] are based on lattice (LWE). NAL15a [22] is based on lattice (NTRU).

Let us take a look at how WDLC10 [7] works. To achieve collusion resilience, WDLC10 uses two key pairs. The core idea of preventing collusion is to use the sum of two secret keys instead of one. This results from the fact that the delegatee and proxy can only work together to obtain the sum of the keys, but cannot learn the value of each secret. The two keys are used for two different layers of ciphertext.

Our scheme achieved collusion resilience with one regular public/secret key pair. Under the general concept of asymmetry encryption, the cleartext can be encrypted with a public key, and the ciphertext is decrypted with the corresponding secret key. However, in the scenario of PRE, we slightly changed the definition. Assuming that anyone can create PRE ciphertext with the given public key, the malicious user could keep the crucial internal value which should be discarded during the encryption. The internal value can be used to generate new re-keys, where the access permission to the ciphertext should be controlled by the owner. In this case, the ciphertext generated with Alice's public key may not actually be controlled by Alice. This may lead to security issues. The proposed scheme uses the secret key for encryption and decryption to ensure that only the owner can create the ciphertext. Alice can generate a re-key with her secret key and Bob's public key.

To summarize, BBS98 [5], Dodis and Ivan [16], and WDLC10 [7] use groups. WDLC10 [7] improved many features compared to BBS98 (including the most important feature, collusion resilience). To archive collusion resilience in "hashed" ElGamal, two key pairs are required for WDLC10 [7]. Shao et al. [17] used double trapdoors. For the other PRE schemes, most of them are based on bilinear pairing or lattice.

3. Preliminaries

We briefly talk about preliminary knowledge for the decentralized storage network and proxy re-encryption.

3.1. Outsourcing Attack and Proof-of-Replication

In a permission-less decentralized storage network, whoever joins the network can provide resources and make incoming attacks. The resource providers may make arbitrary attacks to reduce their costs and increase the margin. One of the most critical is the outsourcing attack. The solution to prevent outsourcing attacks is proof-of-replication [1].

The data must have redundancy stored in a permission-less decentralized storage network. An individual resource provider who deleted the local copy of data to save the storage cost makes an outsourcing attack. When the request to retrieve data comes, the resource provider can fetch the content from another provider and send it back to the requester. The data must be preprocessed into the replication format with the unique key to prevent the outsourcing attack. The cost of replication should be more expensive and time-costly than honestly storing the data. The replicated data are hard for another to utilize, as the replication key is unique. Proof-of-replication ensures the dedicating unique physical store for the data.

3.2. Public Key Encryption

Public key encryption has advantages in key management compared with symmetry key encryption. Users only need to keep their secret keys safe instead of memorizing many passwords. RSA and ElGamal (including ECC) are the most commonly used public key encryption schemes. In RSA, we can either encrypt with a public key or secret key and decrypt with the other, respectively. In ElGamal, the public key is for encryption via Equation (2), and the secret key is for decryption via Equation (3). Public key encryption allows anyone to create an encrypted message and send it to the secret key owner to establish secure communication. We mainly focus on ElGamal here:

$$a, r \in \mathbb{Z}_p, \tag{1}$$

$$pk_A = g^a, \tag{2}$$

$$sk_A = a. \tag{3}$$

where pk_A is the public key, and sk_A is the secret key. Ciphertext c is encrypted with the public key pk_A and the clear message m via Equation (4):

$$c = \langle c_0, c_1 \rangle = \langle g^r, m \cdot pk_A^r \rangle = \langle g^r, m \cdot g^{ar} \rangle. \tag{4}$$

The secret key is required for decryption via Equation (5):

$$m = \frac{c_1}{(c_0)^{sk_A}} = \frac{m \cdot g^{ar}}{(g^r)^a}. \tag{5}$$

The ElGamal scheme satisfies the CPA security. Given the same input m, the output c is different each time according to the random value r. To achieve CCA security, validation is required before the decryption. It detects if the adversary had modified the ciphertext.

3.3. Proxy Re-Encryption

We review the model of collusion-resilience PRE. A CCA collusion-resilience proxy re-encryption scheme is an algorithm:

$$(KeyGen, RenKeyGen, Enc, ReEnc, Dec). \tag{6}$$

KeyGen(): The algorithm generates the public/secret key pair (pk, sk).

ReKeyGen(sk_A, pk_B): The re-encryption key generation algorithm accepts the secret key sk_A of Alice and the public key pk_B of Bob. It outputs a re-encryption key $rk_{A \to B}$.

Enc(sk, m): The encryption algorithm takes the public key sk and the clear message returns the encrypted message c.

ReEnc($rk_{A \to B}, c_A$): The re-encryption algorithm transfers the encrypted message c_A into the ciphertext c_B using the re-encryption key $rk_{A \to B}$. Bob's secret key can decrypt the transformed ciphertext c_B.

Dec(sk, c): The user decrypts the ciphertext with his secret key and encrypted c, e.g., c_A or c_B. It outputs the cleartext m.

Correctness. Correctness is ensured for any $m \in \mathcal{M}$ and any key pair of (pk_A, sk_A), (pk_B, sk_B), following the conditions Equations (7) and (8):

$$Dec(sk_A, Enc(sk_A, m)) = m, \tag{7}$$

$$Dec(sk_B, ReEnc(ReKeyGen(sk_A, pk_B), Enc(sk_A, m))) = m. \tag{8}$$

Security definition. Security for a CCA collusion-resilience PRE scheme is defined in the game between an adversary $\mathcal{A}$ and a challenger $\mathcal{C}$. There are two ciphertexts from the cleartext message for the PRE scheme: encrypted cipher $m \to c_A$ and re-encrypted $m \to c_B$ are required for chosen-ciphertext security.

Phase 1. The adversary $\mathcal{A}$ issues queries $q_1, \ldots, q_m$, of which q_i is one of the following:

- Uncorrupted key generation query: The challenger $\mathcal{C}$ computes $(pk_i, sk_i) \leftarrow KeyGen()$, and sends the pk_i to the adversary $\mathcal{A}$.
- Corrupted key generation query: The challenger $\mathcal{C}$ computes $(pk_j, sk_j) \leftarrow KeyGen()$, and sends the (pk_j, sk_j) to the adversary $\mathcal{A}$.
- Re-encryption key generation query: The challenger $\mathcal{C}$ computes $rk_{1 \to 2} \leftarrow ReKeyGen(sk_1, pk_2)$, and sends the $rk_{1 \to 2}$ to the adversary $\mathcal{A}$. Here, sk_1 and pk_2 must be from different key pairs. This query allows any key pair except that $\mathcal{A}$ cannot know the value of sk_1.
- Re-encryption query: The challenger $\mathcal{C}$ computes $c_2 \leftarrow ReEnc(rk_{1 \to 2}, c_1)$, and sends the ciphertext c_2 to the adversary $\mathcal{A}$.
- Decryption query: The challenger $\mathcal{C}$ computes $m \leftarrow Dec(sk, c)$, and sends the cleartext m to the adversary $\mathcal{A}$. Here, sk cannot be sk_1 or sk_2.

Challenge. After the adversary $\mathcal{A}$ ends up Phase 1, $\mathcal{A}$ chooses from two equal-length messages $m_0, m_1 \in \mathcal{M}$, and sends to the challenger $\mathcal{C}$.

The challenger $\mathcal{C}$ receives m_0, m_1. $\mathcal{C}$ flips a random coin δ Equation (9), and computes c,

$$\delta \leftarrow \{0, 1\}, \tag{9}$$

$$c \leftarrow Enc(sk_A, m_\delta), \tag{10}$$

then sends the c Equation (10) back to the adversary $\mathcal{A}$.

Phase 2. The adversary $\mathcal{A}$ continues to issue queries $q_{m+1}, \ldots, q_{max}$, which q_i can be one of the queries:

- Uncorrupted key generation query: The challenger $\mathcal{C}$ responses are the same as in Phase 1.

- Corrupted key generation query: The challenger $\mathcal{C}$ responses are the same as in Phase 1.
- Re-encryption key generation query: The challenger $\mathcal{C}$ responses are the same as in Phase 1.
- Re-encryption query: The challenger $\mathcal{C}$ responses are the same as in Phase 1.
- Decryption query: The challenger $\mathcal{C}$ responses are the same as in Phase 1, except that $c \neq c_A$ and $sk \neq sk_A$, or $c \neq c_B$ and $sk \neq sk_B$.

Guess. The adversary $\mathcal{A}$ outputs $\hat{\delta} \in \{0, 1\}$.

Referring to adversary $\mathcal{A}$ as an IND-PRE-CCA adversary, we define the advantage of the adversary $\mathcal{A}$ in attacking scheme Π as

$$\mathbf{Adv}_{\Pi,\mathcal{A}}^{IND-PRE-CCA} = |\Pr[\delta = \hat{\delta}] - \frac{1}{2}|. \tag{11}$$

Definition 1. *A PRE scheme Π is said to be $(t, q_u, q_c, q_{rk}, q_{re}, q_d, \epsilon)$-IND-PRE-CCA secure, if for any t-time, IND-PRE-CCA adversary $\mathcal{A}$ makes at most q_u uncorrupted key generation queries, at most q_c corrupted key generation queries, at most q_{rk} re-encryption key generation queries, at most q_{re} re-encryption queries, and at most q_d decryption queries; thus we have*

$$\mathbf{Adv}_{\Pi,\mathcal{A}}^{IND-PRE-CCA} \leq \epsilon. \tag{12}$$

3.4. Complexity Assumptions

The computational assumption of Diffie–Hellman (CDH) is defined as

Definition 2. *$\mathbb{G}$ is a cyclic multiplicative group with prime order p. The CDH problem is said in group $\mathbb{G}$, given a tuple $(g, g^x, g^y) \in \mathbb{G}^3$ with unknown $x, y \leftarrow \mathbb{Z}_p$, to compute g^{xy}.*

A variant of the CDH problem named divisible computation Diffie–Hellman (DCDH) [23] problem is defined as follows.

Definition 3. *Let $\mathbb{G}$ be a cyclic multiplicative group with prime order p. The DCDH problem in group $\mathbb{G}$ is, given $(g, g^{\frac{1}{x}}, g^y) \in \mathbb{G}^3$ with unknown $x, y \leftarrow \mathbb{Z}_p$, to compute g^{xy}.*

The construction of our chosen ciphertext-secure PRE scheme is based on the assumption of modified computational Diffie–Hellman (mCDH). The mCDH problem is a combination of the CDH problem and the DCDH problem.

Definition 4. *Let $\mathbb{G}$ be a cyclic multiplicative group with prime order p. The mCDH problem in group $\mathbb{G}$ is, given a tuple $(g, g^{\frac{1}{x}}, g^x, g^y) \in \mathbb{G}^4$ with unknown $x, y \leftarrow \mathbb{Z}_p$, to compute g^{xy}.*

Definition 5. *For a polynomial time adversary $\mathcal{B}$, the advantage is defined as solving the mCDH problem in group $\mathbb{G}$:*

$$\mathbf{Adv}_{\mathcal{B}}^{mCDH} = \Pr[\mathcal{B}(g, g^{\frac{1}{x}}, g^x, g^y) = g^{xy}]. \tag{13}$$

4. Proxy Re-Encryption Scheme

Our PRE scheme is adopted with the PoRep in a permission-less decentralized storage network. The ciphertext *ReEnc* is an optional operation in the definition. This CCA and collusion-resilience PRE scheme is based on "hashed" ElGamal. ElGamal is one of the most important asymmetry cryptographic schemes based on CDH assumption. Both discrete logarithm and ECC can be used for the ElGamal implementation.

4.1. Features

Collusion resilience. Collusion resilience (collusion safe) states that the proxy and the delegate (Bob) can collude to obtain the delegator's (Alice) secret key. In BBS98 [5],

$rk_{A \to B} = \frac{sk_B}{sk_A}$, proxy and delegate (Bob) can calculate $sk_A = rk_{A \to B} \cdot sk_B$. Collusion resilience (collusion safe) is an important feature. In any case, sk_A should be safe because it is related to more than the current ciphertext. All the ciphertexts generated by Alice are bound with the security of sk_A. Our scheme is collusion resilience due to the novel method of re-key generation, inspired by the bidirectional scheme of Ivan and Dodis [16].

Bidirectional. Delegation from $A \to B$ allows re-encryption from $B \to A$. It is observed that unidirectional and bidirectional delegation can be applied in different use cases. It is nice to distinguish between unidirectional and bidirectional proxy re-encryption. The bidirectional PRE refers to the fact that it can generate $rk_{B \to A}$ from $rk_{A \to B}$. WDLC10 [7] used the two layers for unidirectional encryption, where layer 2 cipher can be converted into layer 1 cipher by $rk_{A \to B} = \frac{\Delta}{sk_{A1} + sk_{A2}}$.

The bidirectional scheme means the re-encrypted ciphertext can transfer back to the original cipher. It depends on how the re-encryption key is designed. In BBS98, $rk_{A \to B} = \frac{sk_B}{sk_A}$ and the reversed key $rk_{B \to A} = \frac{sk_A}{sk_B}$ can be easily calculated. Obviously, this reversed encryption key can be applied to all the ciphertext generated by Bob. In the Ivan and Dodis 2003 bidirectional ElGamal scheme, $rk = g^{r(x_2 - x_1)}$ also can be reversed, but due to the random r, the reversed key can be only applied to Bob's current ciphertext. Comparing the two scenarios, BBS98's bidirectional feature leads to more privacy issues than Ivan and Dodis [16].

Noninteractive. The generation of the re-encryption key requires Alice to use Bob's public key. Bob is not involved in the interaction of re-key generation.

Proxy invisibility. The user sending messages to Alice does not need to be aware of the existence of the proxy. The same applies to Bob, the delegate.

Key optimality. Bob should keep a constant number of secrets, regardless of how many delegations he accepts.

Nontransitive. A proxy re-encryption scheme is transitive if the proxy has right to re-delegate decryption permission. Moreover, it combines several re-encryption keys to produce a new re-key (e.g., from $rk_{A \to B}$ and $rk_{B \to C}$ one can obtain $rk_{A \to C}$). Our scheme is nontransitive, as generating a re-key requires Alice's authorization to prevent transitive action on a proxy.

Transferability. This property, first considered by Ateniese et al. in [18], catches the inability of collusion of the proxy and the delegates to re-delegate decryption rights (i.e., producing new re-encryption keys). The proxy has rk and Bob knows g^r and sk_B, which can generate a new re-key for another user.

4.2. Proposed Scheme

Setup

In the CCA-secure and collusion-resilience PRE scheme, g is the generator of a cyclic multiplicative group $\mathbb{G}$ of prime order p. sk_A Equation (16) is the secret key and pk_A Equation (15) is the public key of Alice. sk_B Equation (18) is the secret key and pk_B Equation (17) is the public key of Bob.

m is the clear message of l_0 bits length in the binary message space denoted by $\mathcal{M}$. m is the random bits of l_1 length. H is the hash function, where $H_1 : \mathbb{Z}_p \cdot \mathbb{Z}_p \to \mathbb{Z}_p$, $H_2 : \{0,1\}^{l_0} \cdot \{0,1\}^{l_1} \to \mathbb{Z}_p$, $H_3 : \mathbb{G}^2 \to \{0,1\}^{l_0 + l_1}$, $H_4 : \mathbb{G} \cdot \{0,1\}^{l_0 + l_1} \to \mathbb{Z}_p$.

KeyGen(): The key generation algorithm generates the public/secret key pair (pk, sk) for the user:

$$a, b \in \mathbb{Z}_p, \qquad (14)$$

$$pk_A = g^a, \qquad (15)$$

$$sk_A = a, \qquad (16)$$

$$pk_B = g^b, \qquad (17)$$

$$sk_B = b. \qquad (18)$$

ReKeyGen(sk_A, pk_B): The re-encryption-key-generating algorithm accepts the secret key sk_A from Alice and the public key pk_B from Bob. The algorithm returns the re-encryption key $rk_{A \to B}$.

Re-key $rk_{A \to B} = (\frac{pk_B}{pk_A})^d = (\frac{g^b}{g^a})^d = g^{bd-ad}$, where the pk_A can be derived from sk_A. When re-encrypting $D_B = D_A \cdot rk_{A \to B} = (g^a)^d \cdot g^{bd-ad} = g^{bd}$, the re-key can only be issued by Alice, who knows $d = H_1(sk_A, r)$.

Enc(sk_A, m): The encryption algorithm takes the secret key sk_A, and the clear message m returns the encrypted message c_A via Equation (19):

$$(m||w) \xrightarrow{Enc} c_A = \langle D_A, r, E, F, V, S \rangle. \tag{19}$$

where $D, r, E, F, V, and S$ are defined as Equations (20)–(24):

$$D_A = (pk_A)^d, d = H_1(sk_A, r), r \leftarrow \mathbb{Z}_p, \tag{20}$$

$$E = g^e, e = H_2(m, w), w \leftarrow \{0,1\}^{l_1}, \tag{21}$$

$$F = H_3(g^d, E) \oplus (m||w), \tag{22}$$

$$V = g^v, v \leftarrow \mathbb{Z}_p, \tag{23}$$

$$S = g^s, s = v + sk_A \cdot r. \tag{24}$$

ReEnc($rk_{A \to B}, c_A$): The re-encryption algorithm transfers the encrypted message c_A into the ciphertext c_B using the generated re-encryption key $rk_{A \to B}$ via Equation (25). Bob's secret key can decrypt the transformed ciphertext c_B. Here, d is used to generate the permission of delegation. Only the content owner can create new D or rk with sk_A and r.

Before the transferring, the validation $S \stackrel{?}{=} V \cdot pk_A^r$ of ciphertext should be checked to ensure Alice generates the ciphertext. Otherwise, the algorithm outputs $\bot$:

$$\begin{aligned} c_A \xrightarrow{ReEnc} c_B &= \langle D_B, r, E, F, V, S \rangle \\ &= \langle D_A \cdot rk_{A \to B}, r, E, F, V, S \rangle. \end{aligned} \tag{25}$$

Dec(sk, c): The user decrypts the ciphertext with his secret key and encrypted c, e.g., c_A or c_B. It outputs the cleartext m and random bits w via Equation (26). After decryption, the validation of ciphertext should be checked $E \stackrel{?}{=} g^{H_2(m,w)}$. If not, the algorithm outputs $\bot$:

$$\begin{aligned} c_B \xrightarrow{Dec} (m||w) &= F \oplus H_3(g^d, E), g^d = D_B^{\frac{1}{sk_B}} \\ &= F \oplus H_3(D_B^{\frac{1}{sk_B}}, E). \end{aligned} \tag{26}$$

In WDLC10 [7], CCA-secure "hashed" ElGamal and modified version is used. The textbook ElGamal is CPA secure and risky in the rounded attack. To enhance the security, "hashed" ElGamal is applied with a message authenticated mechanism.

4.3. Security Analysis

Our collusion-resilience PRE scheme is CCA-secure in a random oracle model, under the modified-computation Diffie–Hellman (mCDH) assumption [24].

In this section, we prove the scheme under mCDH assumption [24] that any efficient algorithm's mCDH advantage is negligible.

Theorem 1. *Our PRE scheme $\prod$ is IND-PRE-CCA-secure under the assumption of the mCDH [24] in group $\mathbb{G}$, and the Schnorr signature [25] is EUF-CMA-secure in the random oracle model. An* adversary $\mathcal{A}$, who asks at most q_{H_i} random oracle queries to H_i with $i \in \{1, \ldots, 4\}$, can effectively break the $(t, q_u, q_c, q_{re}, q_d, \epsilon)$-IND-PRE-CCA of our scheme $\prod$, for any $0 < \nu < \epsilon$. Thus we have:

- The (t', ϵ')-mCDH problem [24] in group $\mathbb{G}$ can be solved by an algorithm $\mathcal{B}$ with Equations (27) and (28):

$$t' \leq t + (q_{H_1} + q_{H_2} + q_{H_3} + q_{H_4}) \\ + q_u + q_c + q_{rk} + q_{re} + q_d)\mathcal{O}(1) \\ + (q_u + q_c + 4q_{re} + 3q_d + (2q_d + q_{re})q_{H_2})t_e, \quad (27)$$

$$\epsilon' \geq \frac{1}{q_{H_3}}(2(\epsilon - \nu) - \frac{q_{H_2} + (q_{H_2} + q_{H_3})q_d}{2^{l_0 + l_1}} - \frac{2q_d + q_{re}}{q}). \quad (28)$$

where t_e is the exponential running time in the group $\mathbb{G}$.
- The EUF-CMA security of the Schnorr signature [25] can be broken by an attacker with advantage ν within time t'.

Proof. It is assumed that the Schnorr signature [25] is (t', ϵ')-EUF-CMA-secure for the probability $0 < \nu < \epsilon$. While the CDH problem (given g, g^x, g^y output g^{xy}) is as hard as the mCDH problem [24] (given $g, g^{\frac{1}{x}}, g^x, g^y$ outputs g^{xy}), this theorem is proved under the mCDH problem [24]. A t-time adversary $\mathcal{A}$ can break the IND-PRE-CCA security of scheme $\prod$ with advantage $\epsilon - \nu$. We show how an algorithm $\mathcal{B}$ solves the (t', ϵ')-mCDH problem [24] in group $\mathbb{G}$. □

Suppose algorithm $\mathcal{B}$ accepts the input of mCDH challenge tuple $(g, g^x, g^{\frac{1}{x}}, g^y) \in \mathbb{G}^4$, and $x, y \leftarrow \mathbb{Z}_p$ is unknown. Algorithm $\mathcal{B}$ plays the role of challenger playing the IND-PRE-CCA game with adversary $\mathcal{A}$. Algorithm $\mathcal{B}$'s goal is to output g^{xy}.

Setup. Algorithm $\mathcal{B}$ passes parameters $(p, \mathbb{G}, g, H_1, H_2, H_3, H_4, l_0, l_1)$ to adversary $\mathcal{A}$. H_1, H_2, H_3, H_4 are random hash oracles controlled by the algorithm $\mathcal{B}$.

Hash Oracle Queries. Adversary $\mathcal{A}$ may send the queries to random oracle H_1, H_2, H_3, and H_4 at any time. Algorithm $\mathcal{B}$ has four empty lists $H_1^{list}, H_2^{list}, H_3^{list}$, and H_4^{list} initially, used for storing the query parameters and result value tuples.

- H_1 queries. With the parameters (a, r), if this query exists in the H_1^{list} as a tuple (a, r, d), output the value d as the result to adversary $\mathcal{A}$. Otherwise, choose $d \leftarrow \mathbb{Z}_p$ and add the tuple (a, r, d) to the hash list H_1^{list}, and respond with $H_1(a, r) = d$ to adversary $\mathcal{A}$.
- H_2 queries. With the parameters (m, w), if this query exists in the H_2^{list} as a tuple (m, w, v), output the value v as the result to adversary $\mathcal{A}$. Otherwise, choose $v \leftarrow \mathbb{Z}_p$ and add the tuple (m, w, v) to the hash list H_2^{list}, and respond with $H_2(m, w) = v$ to adversary $\mathcal{A}$.
- H_3 queries. With the parameters (g^d, E), if this query exists in the H_3^{list} as a tuple (g^d, E, α), output the value α as the result to adversary $\mathcal{A}$. Otherwise, choose $\alpha \leftarrow \{0, 1\}^l$ and add the tuple (g^d, E, α) to the hash list H_3^{list}, and respond with $H_3(g^d, F) = \alpha$ to adversary $\mathcal{A}$.
- H_4 queries. With the parameters (E, F), if this query exists in the H_4^{list} as a tuple (E, F, β), output the value β as the result to adversary $\mathcal{A}$. Otherwise, choose $\beta \leftarrow \mathbb{Z}_p$ and add the tuple (E, F, β) to the hash list H_4^{list}, and respond with $H_4(E, F) = \beta$ to adversary $\mathcal{A}$.

Phase 1. The adversary $\mathcal{A}$ sends a series of queries as in the definition of the IND-PRE-CCA game. The algorithm $\mathcal{B}$ holds three hash lists $K_{Uncorrupted}^{list}$, $K_{Corrupted}^{list}$, and R^{list}, answering the adversary $\mathcal{A}$ as follows:

- Uncorrupted key generation query q_u. If the tuple (a, g^a) is not in the hash list $K_{Uncorrupted}^{list}$, the algorithm $\mathcal{B}$ chooses $a \leftarrow \mathbb{Z}_p$; add the tuple (a, g^a) to the hash list $K_{Uncorrupted}^{list}$. Respond with $pk = g^a$ to adversary $\mathcal{A}$.

- Corrupted key generation query q_c. If the tuple (a, g^a) is not in the hash list $K_{Corrupted}^{list}$, the algorithm $\mathcal{B}$ chooses $a \leftarrow \mathbb{Z}_p$; add the tuple (a, g^a) to the hash list $K_{Corrupted}^{list}$. Respond with $(sk, pk) = (a, g^a)$ to adversary $\mathcal{A}$.
- Re-encryption key generation query q_{rk}. The re-key generation is from Alice's secret key and Bob's public key; both key pairs can be uncorrupted or corrupted. It is because in the re-encryption from c_A to c_B, ciphertexts can be decrypted by either sk_A or sk_B. In the case algorithm, $\mathcal{B}$ recovers $(sk_A, pk_A), (sk_B, pk_B)$ from $K_{Uncorrupted}^{list}$ or $K_{Corrupted}^{list}$. Then, algorithm $\mathcal{B}$ generates re-key $rk_{A \rightarrow B} = (\frac{pk_B}{pk_A})^{H_1(sk_A, r)} = (\frac{g^b}{g^a})^{H_1(a, r)}$. The tuple $(sk_A, pk_A, sk_B, pk_B, rk_{A \rightarrow B})$ is added to the R^{list}. Then, the $rk_{A \rightarrow B}$ is returned to adversary $\mathcal{A}$.

  For the challenge purpose, both sk_A and sk_B should be uncorrupted.
- Re-Encryption query q_{re}. Given $rk_{A \rightarrow B}$ and $c_A = \langle D_A, r, E, F, V, S \rangle$: If $S \neq V \cdot pk_A^r$, it outputs $\bot$. Otherwise, the algorithm returns the re-encrypted ciphertext $c_B = \langle D_A \cdot rk_{A \rightarrow B}, r, E, F, V, S \rangle$ to adversary $\mathcal{A}$.
- Decryption query q_d. The algorithm recovers sk from $K_{Uncorrupted}^{list}$ or $K_{Corrupted}^{list}$. Run $(m, w) = Dec(sk, c)$. If $E = g^{H_2(m, w)}$, give m back to the adversary, otherwise it outputs $\bot$.

Challenge. When adversary $\mathcal{A}$ ends Phase 1, the adversary outputs a target public key pk^* and two equal-length messages $m_0, m_1 \in \{0,1\}^{l_0}$, queries to algorithm $\mathcal{B}$. Algorithm $\mathcal{B}$ responds as follows:

1. Recovers (sk^*, pk^*) from $K_{Uncorrupted}^{list}$ and let $pk^* = g^a := g^{\frac{1}{x}}$.
2. Let $D^* = (pk^*)^d = (g^a)^d := g^y$, so that $(g^a)^d = (g^{\frac{1}{x}})^{xy}$. We can obtain $d = xy$ as $g^a = g^{\frac{1}{x}}$. Then, $g^d = g^{xy}$.
3. As $F = H_3(g^d, E) \oplus (m||w)$ defined, choose $\delta \leftarrow \{0,1\}, w^* \leftarrow \{0,1\}^{l_1}$ and $F^* = H_3(g^d, E^*) \oplus (m_\delta || w^*)$.
4. Return $c^* = \langle D^*, r^*, E^*, F^*, V^*, S^* \rangle$ as the challenged ciphertext to adversary $\mathcal{A}$.

Phase 2. The adversary $\mathcal{A}$ issues the queries as in Phase 1. Algorithm $\mathcal{B}$ responds to those queries to $\mathcal{A}$ as in Phase 1.

Guess. The adversary $\mathcal{A}$ responds a guess $\hat{\delta} \in \{0,1\}$ to $\mathcal{B}$. Algorithm $\mathcal{B}$ calculates $H_3(g^d, E^*) = H_3(g^{xy}, E^*) = F^* \oplus m_{\hat{\delta}} = \hat{\alpha}$. $\mathcal{B}$ looks up the hash list H_3^{list} for the tuple (g^d, E^*, α) where $\alpha = \hat{\alpha}$, then returns the g^d as the solution g^{xy} to the given mCDH instance.

Analysis. First, let us evaluate the simulation of random oracles. H_1, H_4 are perfect As long as $\mathcal{A}$ does not query (m_δ, w) to H_2 or (g^{xy}, E) to H_3, so H_2 and H_3 are perfect. We denote $AskH_2^*$ the event (m_δ, w) has been queried to H_2, and $AskH_3^*$ the event that (g^{xy}, E) has been queried to H_3.

The challenged ciphertext is identically distributed.

Second, the simulation for the re-encryption oracle. The re-encryption query is perfect unless the adversary $\mathcal{A}$ can transfer the ciphertext into the new one without querying hash H_1 to obtain the rk. We denote this event as $ReEncErr$. Since H_1 plays the role of the random oracle, which is queried by adversary $\mathcal{A}$ at most q_{re} times, we have

$$\Pr[ReEncErr] \leq \frac{q_{re}}{q}. \tag{29}$$

Third, the simulation for the decryption oracle. Suppose that $(pk, c), c = (D, r, E, F, V, S)$ is a valid ciphertext, as the validation $S \stackrel{?}{=} V \cdot pk_A^r$ of ciphertext can be checked. There is still a chance that c can be generated by querying other random values to H_3 instead of g^d, where $d = H_1(sk_A, r)$. Denote $Valid$ to be an event that c is valid. Let $AskH_3$ be the event that (g^d, E) has been queried to H_3 and $AskH_2$ be the event that (m, w) has been queried to H_2. Then, we have

$$
\begin{aligned}
&\Pr[Valid|\neg AskH_2] \\
&= \Pr[Valid \wedge AskH_3|\neg AskH_2] \\
&\quad + \Pr[Valid \wedge \neg AskH_3|\neg AskH_2] \\
&\leq \Pr[AskH_3|\neg AskH_2] + \Pr[Valid|\neg AskH_3 \wedge \neg AskH_2] \\
&\leq \frac{q_{H_3}}{2^{l_0+l_1}} + \frac{1}{q},
\end{aligned}
\tag{30}
$$

similarly,

$$
\begin{aligned}
&\Pr[Valid|\neg AskH_3] \\
&= \Pr[Valid \wedge AskH_2|\neg AskH_3] \\
&\quad + \Pr[Valid \wedge \neg AskH_2|\neg AskH_3] \\
&\leq \Pr[AskH_2|\neg AskH_3] + \Pr[Valid|\neg AskH_2 \wedge \neg AskH_3] \\
&\leq \frac{q_{H_2}}{2^{l_0+l_1}} + \frac{1}{q}.
\end{aligned}
\tag{31}
$$

Thus, we have

$$
\begin{aligned}
&\Pr[Valid|\neg AskH_2 \vee \neg AskH_3] \\
&\leq \Pr[Valid|\neg AskH_2] + \Pr[Valid|\neg AskH_3] \\
&\leq \frac{q_{H_2} + q_{H_3}}{2^{l_0+l_1}} + \frac{2}{q}.
\end{aligned}
\tag{32}
$$

Denote *DecErr* as the event that $Valid|(\neg AskH_2 \vee \neg AskH_3)$ happens during the entire simulation. The q_d times of decryption queries have been issued to a decryption oracle, and we have

$$
\Pr[DecErr] \leq \frac{(q_{H_2} + q_{H_3})q_d}{2^{l_0+l_1}} + \frac{2q_d}{q}.
\tag{33}
$$

Denote *Good* as the event $AskH_3^* \vee (AskH_2^*|\neg AskH_3^*) \vee ReEncErr \vee DecErr$. If *Good* has not happened, the adversary $\mathcal{A}$ cannot gain any advantage in guessing δ from m_0, m_1, due to the random E as one of the input of $H_3(g^d, E)$ and $E = g^e = g^{H_2(m,w)}$ is generated with the random bits $w \leftarrow \{0,1\}^{l_1}$. We have $\Pr[\delta = \delta'|\neg Good] = \frac{1}{2}$

$$
\begin{aligned}
&\Pr[\delta = \delta'] \\
&= \Pr[\delta = \delta'|\neg Good]\Pr[\neg Good] + \Pr[\delta = \delta'|Good]\Pr[Good] \\
&\leq \frac{1}{2}\Pr[\neg Good] + \Pr[Good] \\
&= \frac{1}{2}(1 - \Pr[Good]) + \Pr[Good] \\
&= \frac{1}{2} + \frac{1}{2}\Pr[Good],
\end{aligned}
\tag{34}
$$

and

$$
\begin{aligned}
&\Pr[\delta = \delta'] \\
&\geq \Pr[\delta = \delta'|\neg Good]\Pr[\neg Good] \\
&= \frac{1}{2}(1 - \Pr[Good]) \\
&= \frac{1}{2} - \frac{1}{2}\Pr[Good],
\end{aligned}
\tag{35}
$$

we have

$$|\Pr[\delta = \delta'] - \frac{1}{2}| \leq \frac{1}{2}\Pr[Good]. \tag{36}$$

By the definition, the advantage $(\epsilon - \nu)$ for IND-PRE-CCA adversary:

$$\begin{aligned}
\epsilon - \nu &= |\Pr[\delta = \delta'] - \frac{1}{2}| \\
&\leq \frac{1}{2}\Pr[Good] \\
&= \frac{1}{2}(\Pr[AskH_3^* \vee (AskH_2^*|\neg AskH_3^*) \vee ReEncErr \vee DecErr]) \\
&= \frac{1}{2}(\Pr[AskH_3^*] + \Pr[AskH_2^*|\neg AskH_3^*] \\
&\quad + \Pr[ReEncErr] + \Pr[DecErr]).
\end{aligned} \tag{37}$$

Since $\Pr[ReEncErr] \leq \frac{q_{re}}{q}$, $\Pr[DecErr] \leq \frac{(q_{H_2}+q_{H_3})q_d}{2^{l_0+l_1}} + \frac{2q_d}{q}$ and $\Pr[AskH_2^*|\neg AskH_3^*] \leq \frac{q_{H_2}}{2^{l_0+l_1}}$, we obtain

$$\begin{aligned}
\Pr[AskH_3^*] &\geq 2(\epsilon - \nu) - [AskH_2^*|\neg AskH_3^*] \\
&\quad - \Pr[DecErr] - \Pr[ReEncErr] \\
&\geq 2(\epsilon - \nu) - \frac{q_{H_2}}{2^{l_0+l_1}} \\
&\quad - \frac{(q_{H_2}+q_{H_3})q_d}{2^{l_0+l_1}} - \frac{2q_d}{q} - \frac{q_{re}}{q} \\
&= 2(\epsilon - \nu) - \frac{q_{H_2} + (q_{H_2}+q_{H_3})q_d}{2^{l_0+l_1}} - \frac{2q_d + q_{re}}{q}.
\end{aligned} \tag{38}$$

In event $AskH_3^*$, algorithm $\mathcal{B}$ will be able to solve the mCDH instance, and, consequentially, the following is obtained:

$$\epsilon' \geq \frac{1}{q_{H_3}}(2(\epsilon - \nu) - \frac{q_{H_2} + (q_{H_2}+q_{H_3})q_d}{2^{l_0+l_1}} - \frac{2q_d + q_{re}}{q}). \tag{39}$$

From the description of the simulation, the running time of algorithm $\mathcal{B}$ can be bounded by

$$\begin{aligned}
t' &\leq t + (q_{H_1} + q_{H_2} + q_{H_3} + q_{H_4} \\
&\quad + q_u + q_c + q_{rk} + q_{re} + q_d)\mathcal{O}(1) \\
&\quad + (q_u + q_c + 4q_{re} + 3q_d + (2q_d + q_{re})q_{H_2})t_e.
\end{aligned} \tag{40}$$

This completes the proof of Theorem 1.

5. Experiment

In this section, we analyze the computation cost. With the development of the blockchain in the past decade, elliptic curves cryptography (ECC), including ECDSA and 25519, has become the standard user access credential. The group with big integers is less used nowadays. As ECC computation is still heavy even for a modern CPU, we propose the practical implementation which cached the ECC operation to speed up for practice. Otherwise, the encryption and decryption over ECC would take too long a time and become meaningless.

5.1. Schemes Comparison

The two group-based schemes without pairings are using double trapdoors [26] and "hashed: ElGamal [7]. In Table 1, the comparison results indicate that the proposed scheme is slower than WDLC10 for encryption, since "hashed" ElGamal is used. Our scheme does not differentiate the first and the second level of ciphertext. t_{eN} is the time in exponential operation over the N^2 group, where N is the safe prime. Let $N = pq$ be a safe prime modulus, such that $p = 2p' + 1$, $q = 2q' + 1$, and p, p', q, q' are primes. t_e is the time in exponential operation over the group. k is the length of generated key in $KeyGen(1^k)$. k_1 is the hash algorithm $H : \{0,1\}^* \to \{0,1\}^{k_1}$. N_x and N_y are the safe-prime modulus corresponding to the delegator and the delegatee, respectively. The ReEnc is not available in our scheme as we do not transfer the ciphertext, but it only generates a re-key.

Table 1. Comparison with Shao09 and WDLC10.

	Schemes	Shao09	WDLC10	Ours
Compute Cost	ReKenGen	$2t_{eN}$	t_e	t_e
	Enc	$5t_{eN}$	$3t_e$	$5t_e$
	Dec	$4t_{eN}$	$3t_e$	$2t_e$
	ReEnc	$5t_{eN}$	$3t_e$	N/A
Ciphertext Size	1st level	$2k + 3\|N_x^2\| + \|m\|$	$3\|\mathbb{G}\|$	$4\|\mathbb{G}\| + \|m\| + \|w\|$
	2nd level	$k_1 + 3\|N_x^2\| + 2\|N_y^2\| + \|m\|$	$3\|\mathbb{G}\| + \|\mathbb{Z}_q\|$	
Security	Security Level	collusion resistant, CCA	collusion resistant, CCA	collusion resistant, CCA
	Standard model	Yes	Yes	Yes
	Underlying Assumptions	DDH	CDH	CDH

5.2. Practical Implementation

Due to the computation inefficiency of ECC, in the practical implementation, we can use elliptic curves and cyclic multiplicative group together to boost the encryption.

For the practical encryption and decryption, the message is divided into small chunks m, as each time that group operation is involved in the computation, using ECC will cost much longer time. For the calculation $F = H_3(g^d, E) \oplus (m||w)$, where $E = g^e$, $e = H_2(m, w)$, $w \leftarrow \{0,1\}^{l_1}$, the operation $E = g^e$ will be too expensive if using ECC. On the other hand, ECC provides better security with less secret key length in bits for the user's public key and secret key. Roughly speaking, 160 bits of the ECC secret key are as strong as 1024 bits of the secret key required in RSA or ElGamal over the multiplicative integer group.

It is better to divide and conquer the problem by using both the elliptic curves group and the cyclic multiplicative integer group $g \in \mathbb{G}_p$. In the calculation $D_A = (pk_A)^d$, $d = H_1(sk_A, r)$, $r \leftarrow \mathbb{Z}_p$, for the user key pair (pk, sk), we use generator $g_{ECC} \in \mathbb{G}_{ECC}$, then $pk = g_{ECC}^{sk}$. Meanwhile $F = H_3(g^d, E) \oplus (m||w)$ the exponential operation g^d in H_3 can be calculated only once in ECC and cached. Another exponential calculation $E = g^e$ must be evaluated for every m and w. Thus, for g^n, the ECC operation will be too heavy. Here, we have the modification below:

$$(m||w) \xrightarrow{Enc} c_A = \langle D_A, r, E, F, V, S \rangle. \tag{41}$$

where D, r, E, F, V, S is defined as:

$$D_A = (pk_A)^d, d = H_1(sk_A, r), r \leftarrow \mathbb{Z}_p, \tag{42}$$

$$E = g^e, e = H_2(m, w), w \leftarrow \{0,1\}^{l_1}, \tag{43}$$

$$F = H_3(g_{ECC}^d, E) \oplus (m||w), \tag{44}$$

$$V = g_{ECC}^v, v \leftarrow \mathbb{Z}_p, \tag{45}$$

$$S = g_{ECC}^s, s = v + sk_A \cdot r. \tag{46}$$

For the re-encryption $c_A \xrightarrow{ReEnc} c_B$, re-encrypting $D_B = D_A \cdot rk_{A \to B} = (g_{ECC}^a)^d \cdot g_{ECC}^{bd-ad} = g_{ECC}^{bd}$, where re-key $rk_{A \to B} = (\frac{pk_B}{pk_A})^d = (\frac{g_{ECC}^b}{g_{ECC}^a})^d = g_{ECC}^{bd-ad}$. For the validation $E \stackrel{?}{=} g^{H_2(m,w)}$ after decryption, as pk is not involved, no ECC operation needs to be performed.

5.3. Performance Comparison

Python 3.8 is used to implement our PRE scheme and WDLC10. Since Shao09 uses a different theory over the large prime numbers, it was hard to make a fair comparison by choosing the parameters. The code is modified from an open-source pure Python library named python-ecdsa, which is licensed in the public domain.

We implemented the ECC version of our PRE scheme and the practical modification in Python 3.8 and tested it on a MacBook Air of Intel Core i5 at a processor speed of 1.3 GHz. For every 64 bytes of data (including 48 bytes clear message m and 16 bytes of random initialization vector w), we repeat encryption 100 thousand times and note the time cost.

Our scheme is slightly slower than WDLC10 for encrypting in theory, as we described in Table 1. However, for the modification for practical cached exponential operation for g_{ECC}, from Figure 4, we can observe that practical modification can speed up the encryption by avoiding ECC computation. In most cases, elliptic curve-based asymmetry cryptography is commonly used in the signature or key exchange due to its slowness. However, the decentralized storage network shows the scenarios where an asymmetry encryption is required. Meanwhile, it is nice to have the key strength and reasonable encryption/decryption speed. The result of Figure 4 shows that even for a modern CPU, the computation is insufficient for fast encryption. The practical implementation is helpful to speed up the operation while maintaining the security from ECC with less key length.

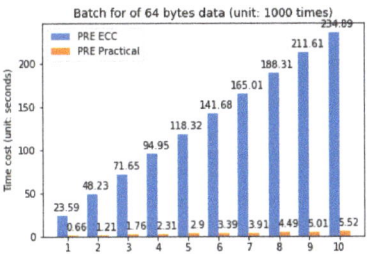

Figure 4. Time cost for PRE ECC and practical encryption for every 1000 times of encryption of 64 bytes data on MacBook 1.3 GHz Intel Core i5.

In the experiment, we use the cyclic multiplicative group over an integer of 196 bits for both ours and WDLC10. The ECC curve is NIST192p. The message m size is 48 bytes and w is 16 bytes since the blake2b outputs up to 64 bytes (512 bits) each time.

In Figure 5, we compare our practical modification PRE scheme with pure-Python-implemented WDLC10. PRE brings useful access control, privacy features, and better key management than symmetry encryption. Unlike WDLC10, there is no requirement for layer 1 and layer 2 ciphertext. Our scheme needs only one public/secret key pair. For the hash function, we use blake2b, which can output a flexible length of the hash digest. For the curve, we use NIST192p. Our proxy re-encryption is ready for practice. Figure 5 shows that with the modification on our scheme, the ECC computing is cached, so our scheme can be slightly faster than WDLC10 even if the theory shows our scheme was slower, shown in Table 1.

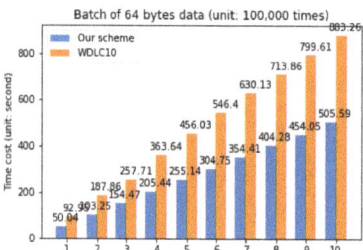

Figure 5. Time cost for our PRE scheme and WDLC10 encryption for every 100 k times of encryption of 64 bytes data on MacBook 1.3 GHz Intel Core i5.

5.4. Performance on the Embedded Device

The PRE encryption and decryption are highly likely to be performed on an embedded device, such as an IP camera or mobile phone. Figure 6 shows the performance of our PRE scheme and WDLC10 on an early model of Raspberry Pi microcomputer. The early version of Raspberry Pi has quite low computation capacity; however, it achieves a reasonable performance. In addition, the permission grant in our scheme does not require transfer of the ciphertext, which would be friendly to the embedded devices. Recently, the embed device has attained a faster CPU with multi-cores. The feature of skipping the re-encryption makes it fit better for the embedded device.

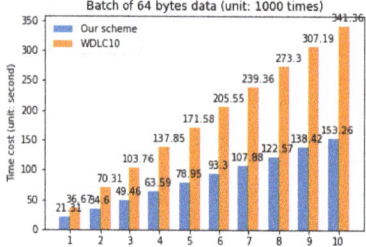

Figure 6. Time cost for our PRE scheme and WDLC10 encryption for every 1000 times of encryption of 64 bytes data on a 1st generation of Raspberry Pi model B 700 Hz.

6. Evaluation

6.1. Remove Access or Corrupted Ciphertext

Thus far, our scheme covers the encryption and decryption of data and shares the data with the public key of another user. We can either choose to generate a $rk_{A \to B}$ or D_B, and it is possible to generate a new ciphertext by replacing D_B with D_A or reuse c_A by placing D_B in a separate file.

$$c_A \xrightarrow{ReEnc} c_B$$

How about removing the access permission of a user? The concept of forwarding secrecy [27] was introduced in cryptography. Strictly, since a message is sent to another one, it is not a secret anymore, as the content could be copied and shared again. It is impossible to revoke a message or erase information with cryptography. However, in practice, people come and leave the organization, and granting or revoking data access permission is the daily operation. If a user intends to expose the critical information g_{ECC}^d to the public, the cipher c is no longer a secret. In those cases, the cryptography method can not ensure security in practice. The only choice is to remove the existing ciphertext to prevent further information leaking.

We provide another ciphertext transfer operation. It is not a part of our scheme but it is useful when transferring the ciphertext into a new one when the message is leaking, and this operation could be applied after any data access permission is revoked.

Transfer operation $c_A \xrightarrow{Transfer} c'_A$, where $c'_A = \langle D'_A, r', E, F', V', S' \rangle$:

$$D'_A = (pk_A)^{d'}, d' = H_1(sk_A, r'), r' \leftarrow \mathbb{Z}_p, \quad (47)$$

$$\begin{aligned} F' &= F \oplus re \\ &= F \oplus H_3(g^d, E) \oplus H_3(g^{d'}, E) \\ &= H_3(g^d, E) \oplus (m||w) \oplus H_3(g^d, E) \oplus H_3(g^{d'}, E) \\ &= H_3(g^{d'}, E) \oplus (m||w), \end{aligned} \quad (48)$$

$$V' = g^{v'}, v' \leftarrow \mathbb{Z}_p, \quad (49)$$

$$S' = g^{s'}, s' = v' + sk_A \cdot r'. \quad (50)$$

The ciphertext transfering key re is defined:

$$re = H_3(g^d, E) \oplus H_3(g^{d'}, E). \quad (51)$$

It is safe to send the transfer key to the proxy and transfer the existing ciphertext into a new one. By this operation, the previous ciphertext is discarded, and the new permission of access should be regenerated.

The concept above is also helpful in blockchain storage content for key renewal. Periodically changing the secret key is recommended to avoid potential confidential key leakage. A finance blockchain such as Bitcoin can create another secret/public key pair and transfer existing coin assets to the new wallet address. The signature is the evidence of a coin transaction. As opposed to this, the storage blockchain uses a secret key to decrypt. Losing a key is losing the data unless an algorithm can transfer the old ciphertext to the new one under the new key. Our PRE scheme is suitable for this scenario.

6.2. Search with PRE

The commercial applications are interested in searching [28,29]. Nowadays, searching in data is more than just full-text matching. Complexity algorithms are applied to texts, images, videos, and even speech. A CPA-secure encryption works against searching over the ciphertext in concept. Even if, in the future, the full homomorphic encryption [30] is ready, it might be hard to perform a search over CPA ciphertexts.

With proxy re-encryption, it is possible to design the application that outsources the information processing to the trusted party. Data could be stored safely on the cloud with versions, and the index for the recent version will be processed in-house.

6.3. Applications with PRE

We introduced PRE for decentralized storage network scenarios, which are the fundamental components for lots of blockchain applications. It is possible to build a media store for movies and music based on blockchain. Once a user purchases the movie, he has the right to download the movie file content freely. A purchase record is marked on the blockchain, as evidence of the right to use from the intellectual property owner. It is publicly verifiable. The PRE re-key can be used as evidence. The evidence can be listed publicly and it is meaningful only to the purchaser who owns the secret key.

7. Conclusions

In this paper, we proposed a PRE scheme satisfying the PoRep scenario. Since the PoRep is the key algorithm for a decentralized storage network, the proposed PRE would be an important candidate for a future blockchain storage network. In a decentralized storage network, access control must be cryptography-based. Meanwhile, the decentralized storage network suffers from outsourcing attacks. Proof-of-replication helps to convince users that their content is kept by the dedicated storage resource. The proposed PRE scheme is suited for proof-of-replication, which does not generate the extra ciphertext. The scheme reduces the cost of cryptographic access control. Moreover, our PRE scheme is CCA-secure and only requires one key pair. With the practical implementation, it is reasonably fast to use in applications.

Nowadays, users become used to placing their data on the public cloud. Although the data access is permission-controlled, it might be transparent to cloud storage providers. Employing the PRE scheme will bring true privacy to user data, even if the service provider is semi-trusted.

Due to the computation efficiency, symmetry encryption is widely used for encryption. However, the key management for symmetry encryption is complex, leading to more privacy issues. With the maturity of the PRE scheme, it can bring more flexibility to data storage and access control. Asymmetry encryption will play a more important role in blockchain-based systems.

8. Future Work

In this paper, we proposed the proxy re-encryption for the decentralized storage networks. It is a CCA-secure, collusion-resilience PRE scheme that requires only one key pair. The PRE scheme works under the concept of proof-of-replication, which is the core algorithm of the decentralized storage network, and the proposed scheme is reasonable, fast, and practical. It can be used for mobile and IoT devices. In the future, we will keep working on speeding up the scheme. Furthermore, it is possible to add more features based on the current scheme, e.g., the multiply public keys re-encryption, or the time-limited re-key issuing. To enable searching within PRE is also an interesting topic.

Author Contributions: Funding acquisition, D.L.; Supervision, X.H.; Writing—original draft, J.K.; Writing—review & editing, J.Z. All authors have read and agreed to the published version of the manuscript.

Funding: This research was funded in part by the XJTLU Key Program Special Fund under grant number KSF-E-05. This work is supported by Research Project Supported by Shanxi Scholarship Council of China 2021-038, and Applied Basic Research Project of Shanxi Province No. 20210302123130, No. 20210302124273. This work was partially supported by the National Natural Science Foundation of China under Grant No. 62002296; the Natural Science Foundation of Jiangsu Province under Grant No. BK20200250; and the XJTLU Key Programme Special Fund under Grant No. KSF-E-54.

Conflicts of Interest: The authors declare no conflict of interest.

Glossaries

pk	The public key is a part of the key pair. The pk is a big integer internally.
sk	The secret key is a part of the key pair. The sk is a generator of a multiplicative group or the generator point in ECC.
rk	The re-key rk is from the concept of proxy re-encryption, which converts the ciphertext c_A encrypted by Alice's pk_A to a new ciphertext c_B which can be decrypted with Bob's sk_B. The $rk_{A \to B}$ is generated under Alice's permission. It requires Alice's sk_A and Bob's pk_B to generate $rk_{A \to B}$.
M	is the message space that contains all the combinations of message m.
m	is the clear message which will be encrypted. It is represented in binary in length l. In our scheme, we have $m \in \{0,1\}^{l_0}$.
w	is the random bits of length l_1 generated when encrypting message m. This provides CPA-level security that the same message will output different ciphertext under multiple times of encryption.

l	is the message length in bits. We have $l = l_0 + l_1$, where l_0 is the length of m and l_1 is the length of w.
c	is the ciphertext. In proxy re-encryption, beside encryption and decryption, the ciphertext c_A can be transferred to another ciphertext c_B with the $rk_{A \to B}$ under Alice(A)'s permission grant.
d	is the hash value generated by user Alice's secret key sk_A and the random integer r. d is an important value during the calculation which needs to be discarded to keep the ciphertext safe. Otherwise, g^d can be used for decryption without a secret key.
D	is the first element of the ciphertext. When decrypting, g^d will be calculated from D with sk, and when re-encrypting, $rk_{A \to B}$ is applied to D_A to obtain D_B as $D_B = D_A \cdot rk_{A \to B}$.
r	is the second element of the ciphertext. The random r makes sure the value d is random.
E	is a part of the ciphertext. E is calculated from m and w. It is a signature used for satisfying the CCA security. This signature $E \stackrel{?}{=} g^{H_2(m,w)}$ will be checked after decryption by the user to verify m.
F	is a part of the ciphertext. The concatenation of message m and w is hidden in F. Value g^d is required for encryption or decryption.
v	is a random value used in the Schnorr signature. It is an internal value, which needs to be discarded to keep the secret key safe in s.
V	is a part of the ciphertext. Together with s and pk, it performs the Schnorr signature check before re-encryption.
s	is used for Schnorr's signature to verify the identity of who encrypts the ciphertext. s is hiding in $S = g^s$ to stay safe. Even if m is too long and split into $m = m_1\|\|m_2\|\|...\|\|m_i$, the v and s only need to generate once.
S	is the last element of the ciphertext. It is a value for Schnorr's signature. This signature $S \stackrel{?}{=} V \cdot pk_A^r$ will be checked before re-encrypting c by the proxy.
H	is the hash function. The hash function is a one-way function, which is easy to calculate the function's output from the input value, but it is hard to obtain the input from the given output. In our scheme, we have H_1, H_2, H_3, and H_4, which take different types of input and return different outputs. $H_1 : \mathbb{G} \cdot \mathbb{Z}_p \to \mathbb{Z}_p$, $H_2 : \{0,1\}^{l_0} \cdot \{0,1\}^{l_1} \to \mathbb{Z}_p$, $H_3 : \mathbb{G}^2 \to \{0,1\}^{l_0+l_1}$, $H_4 : \mathbb{G} \cdot \{0,1\}^{l_0+l_1} \to \mathbb{Z}_p$. In practice, those H functions can use any standard hash function such as sha2 or blake2b with data type converting between bytes and integer.
CDH	is computational Diffie–Hellman (CDH) assumption. The CDH problem in group $\mathbb{G}$ is, given a tuple $(g, g^x, g^y) \in \mathbb{G}^3$ with unknown $x, y \leftarrow \mathbb{Z}_p$, to compute g^{xy}.
mCDH	is the modified computational Diffie–Hellman (mCDH) assumption. Given a tuple $(g, g^{\frac{1}{x}}, g^x, g^y) \in \mathbb{G}^4$ with unknown $x, y \leftarrow \mathbb{Z}_p$, it is hard to compute g^{xy}.
g	In our PRE scheme, g stands for the generator of the multiplicative group.
g_{ECC}	In our PRE scheme, g_{ECC} stands for the generator point of the group of the elliptic curve (ECC).
$\mathbb{Z}_p$	is the non-negative integer set less than a prime integer p, and p is the prime order of a cyclic multiplicative group.
Adversary $\mathcal{A}$	is an efficient adversary who attempts to solve the problem in the security game. Adversary $\mathcal{A}$ issues the queries to the challenger $\mathcal{C}$, and the challenger responds.
Algorithm $\mathcal{B}$	is an algorithm which can break the mCDH problem. In a security reduction, adversary $\mathcal{A}$ transforms the existing problem to the mCDH problem, which algorithm $\mathcal{B}$ can solve, to show the hardness of security.
Challenger $\mathcal{C}$	is the role in the security game that responds to adversary $\mathcal{A}$'s queries following CCA-secure rules.
K^{list}	is a hash list used to simulate the random oracle behavior. The algorithm $\mathcal{B}$ maintains two hash list $K^{list}_{Uncorrupted}$, $K^{list}_{Corrupted}$ and R^{list}, answering the adversary $\mathcal{A}$'s queries.
H^{list}	is a hash list used to simulate the random oracle behavior. Algorithm $\mathcal{B}$ has four lists $H^{list}_1, H^{list}_2, H^{list}_3$, and H^{list}_4, answering the adversary $\mathcal{A}$'s queries.

References

1. Benet, J.; Dalrymple, D.; Greco, N. *Proof of Replication*; Protocol Labs: San Francisco, CA, USA, 2017.
2. Fisch, B. *PoReps: Proofs of Space on Useful Data*; Protocol Labs: San Francisco, CA, USA, 2018.
3. Fisch, B.; Bonneau, J.; Greco, N.; Benet, J. *Scaling proof-of-replication for Filecoin Mining*; Protocol Labs: San Francisco, CA, USA, 2018.
4. Kan, J. Economic Proof of Work. In *Cryptology ePrint Archive*; Report 2020/1117; Springer: Berlin/Heidelberg, Germany, 2020.
5. Blaze, M.; Bleumer, G.; Strauss, M.J. Divertible protocols and atomic proxy cryptography. In *Theory and Application of Cryptographic Techniques*; Springer: Berlin/Heidelberg, Germany, 1998; pp. 127–144.
6. Elgamal, T. A public key cryptosystem and a signature scheme based on discrete logarithms. *IEEE Trans. Inf. Theory* **1985**, *31*, 469–472. [CrossRef]
7. Weng, J.; Deng, R.H.; Liu, S.; Chen, K. Chosen-ciphertext secure bidirectional proxy re-encryption schemes without pairings. *Inf. Sci.* **2010**, *180*, 5077–5089. [CrossRef]
8. Ran, C.; Susan, H. Chosen-ciphertext secure proxy reencryption. In Proceedings of the 14th ACM Conference on Computer and Communications Security, Alexandria, VA, USA, 2 November–31 October 2007; pp. 185–194.
9. Benoît, L.; Damien, V. Unidirectional chosen-ciphertext secure proxy re-encryption. Information Theory. *IEEE Trans.* **2011**, *57*, 1786–1802.
10. Chu, C.-K.; Tzeng, W.-G. *Identity-Based proxy re-encryption without Random Oracles*; Springer: Berlin/Heidelberg, Germany, 2007.
11. Toshihiko, M. Proxy re-encryption systems for identity-based encryption. In *Pairing-Based Cryptography–Pairing 2007*; Springer: Berlin/Heidelberg, Germany, 2007; pp. 247–267.
12. Giuseppe, A.; Karyn, B.; Susan, H. *Key-Private proxy re-encryption*; Springer: Berlin/Heidelberg, Germany, 2009.
13. Elena Kirshanova. Proxy re-encryption from lattices. In P*ublic-Key Cryptography–PKC 2014*; Springer: Berlin/Heidelberg, Germany, 2004; pp. 77–94.
14. Satoshi, N. Bitcoin: A peer-to-peer electronic cash system. *Decentralized Bus. Rev.* **2008**, 21260.
15. Dwork, C.; Naor, M. Pricing via Processing or Combatting Junk Mail. In *International Cryptology Conference*; Springer: Berlin/Heidelberg, Germany, 1992.
16. Ivan, A.; Dodis, Y. Proxy Cryptography Revisited. In *Network and Distributed System Security Symposium*; Springer: Berlin/Heidelberg, Germany, 2003.
17. Nuez, D.; Agudo, I.; Lopez, J. proxy re-encryption. *J. Netw. Comput. Appl.* **2017**, *87*, 193–209. [CrossRef]
18. Ateniese, G.; Fu, K.; Green, M.; Hohenberger, S. Improved proxy re-encryption schemes with applications to secure distributed storage. *ACM Trans. Inf. Syst. Secur.* **2006**, *9*, 1–30. [CrossRef]
19. Green, M.; Ateniese, G. Identity-Based Proxy Re-encryption. In *Applied Cryptography and Network Security*; Springer: Berlin/Heidelberg, Germany, 2007; 288–306.
20. Keita, X.; Keisuke, T. Proxy re-encryption based on learning with errors. In Proceedings of the 2010 Symposium on Cryptography and Information Security, Amalfi, Italy, 13–15 September 201 0.
21. Yoshinori, A.; Xavier, B.; Le Trieu, P.; Lihua, W. Keyprivate proxy re-encryption under LWE. In *Progress in Cryptology–INDOCRYPT 2013*; Springer: Cham, Switzerland, 2013; pp. 1–18.
22. David, N.; Isaac, A.; Javier, L. NTRUReEncrypt: An efficient proxy re-encryption scheme based on NTRU. In Proceedings of the 10th ACM Symposium on Information, Computer and Communications Security, ASIA CCS '15, New York, NY, USA, 14–17 April 2015; pp. 179–189.
23. Bao, F.; Deng, R.H.; Zhu, H. Variations of Diffie-Hellman Problem. In *International Conference on Information and Communication Security*; Springer: Berlin/Heidelberg, Germany, 2003.
24. Libert, B.; Vergnaud, D. Multi-use unidirectional proxy re-signatures. In Proceedings of the 15th ACM Conference on Computer and Communications Security, Alexandria, VA, USA, 27–31 October 2008.
25. Schnorr, C. Efficient Identification and Signatures for Smart Cards. In *International Cryptology Conference*; Springer: New York, NY, USA, 1989.
26. Shao, J.; Cao, Z. CCA-Secure Proxy Re-encryption without Pairings. In *Public Key Cryptography*; Springer: Berlin/Heidelberg, Germany, 2009; pp. 357–376.
27. Derler, D.; Krenn, S.; Lorünser, T.; Ramacher, S.; Slamanig, D.; Striecks, C. Revisiting Proxy Re-encryption: Forward Secrecy, Improved Security, and Applications. In Proceedings of the Public-Key Cryptography, Rio de Janeiro, Brazil, 25–29 March 2018; pp. 219–250.
28. Boneh, D. *Public Key Encryption with Keyword Search*; Springer: Berlin/Heidelberg, Germany, 2004.
29. Kamara, S.; Lauter, K.E. *Cryptographic Cloud Storage*; Financial Cryptography; Springer: Berlin/Heidelberg, Germany, 2010.
30. Van Dijk, M.; Gentry, C.; Halevi, S.; Vaikuntanathan, V. Fully homomorphic encryption over the integers. In *Theory and Application of Cryptographic Techniques*; Springer: Berlin/Heidelberg, Germany, 2010.

MDPI
St. Alban-Anlage 66
4052 Basel
Switzerland
Tel. +41 61 683 77 34
Fax +41 61 302 89 18
www.mdpi.com

Applied Sciences Editorial Office
E-mail: applsci@mdpi.com
www.mdpi.com/journal/applsci